SAFER JAIL AND PRISON MATTERS

Effective Ways To Manage and Reduce Violence in Correctional Facilities

Elvis Slaughter

ISBN: 978-0-9965932-5-0

Library of Congress Control Number: 2016912372

(S & A) Publishing

Elvis Slaughter

P. O. Box 314

Calumet City, IL 60409

For information about bulk purchase, please contact (S & A) Publishing.

Eslaugh108@aol.com

www.safer-jail-and-prison-matters.com.

Printed in the United States of America

Dedication

I will not fail to mention that I was blessed to have worked at Cook County Sheriff's office, where the staff challenged and inspired me throughout my career. I dedicate this work to the Cook County Sheriff's Office. I have also been greatly blessed and therefore indebted to several authors that have contributed to the success of my career: Napoleon Hill, Steven R. Covey and Claude Bristol. I am also indebted to the Illinois Academy of Criminology and the late Mary Powers, who embodies the philosophy and stance of Citizens Alert on public issues and unwaveringly on criminal justice accountability, and my personal attorney and legal advisor, the late William Thomas "Tom" Huyck, who was a former prosecutor for both the U.S. Department of Justice and the U.S. Attorney's office. He also successfully argued a case before the U.S. Supreme Court, (Liparota v. United States). Tom and Mary were caring and passionate about all people and civil justice. They all provided thoughtful suggestions which I incorporated in the practices at the correctional facility as I rose through the ranks from officer to superintendent. I have been blessed with a lovely family, and I am indeed grateful to my wife and the Slaughter family for helping me raise three wonderful children, who encouraged me to make tough decisions during challenging moments. I know I would never have done it without your support and love, and I am grateful for your blessings. Thank you all.

Contents

Prologue

"We cannot emphasize enough the importance of both professionalism and respect for human rights."

President Nelson Mandela speaking to prison staff in South Africa in 1998

In 1984, the last visitor had just exited the facility and things seemed like every other day in the facility, until suddenly the alarm sounded. I was startled and caught off guard, because I have not had such an experience before, neither was I expecting any incident like that. Two armed inmates that were charged with murder attempted to escape from the correctional facility. They had already taken an officer hostage and were dressed in staff uniforms. By securing the gate, I was able to prevent them from escaping from the facility with an unloaded shotgun. Indeed, it is a day I will live to remember all my life.

After this dangerous encounter with the inmates, I encountered sleepless nights, wondering about the possibilities of another dangerous encounter. It was a moment of epiphany on how knowledge, experience and fear could make or break an individual. After that encounter, my attitude towards safety and security changed, as I ensured that such a traumatic experience would never occur again. I have had real experiences and acquired good knowledge through research that I intend to share with every organization and correctional officer ready to prepare for the unknown, and determined to succeed in their careers.

Safer Jail and Prison Matters is a guidebook for the correctional institutions that offers evidence-based insights that can positively enhance the practices at correctional institutions and law enforcement agencies. Most organizations that operate without a definite plan and in uncertain environments will greatly benefit from established practices within a system approach. It provides every correctional officer and law enforcement service with answers to some of the greatest questions and issues that they face daily in the execution of their duties.

Introduction

"It is his capacity for self-improvement and self-redemption which most distinguishes man from the mere brute." Aung San Suu Kyi, Freedom from Fear

I would not forget my very first day as an officer at the Cook County Sheriff's Office. I was distraught. I was in a tier with fifty inmates, which included murderers, and I was just twenty-three. I really needed mentoring or training to assist me on the job, but in those days, there was no training or mentoring within the first few months, and there were no supervisors around to help. While I was contemplating my next course of action, an inmate introduced himself to me and also taught me the daily routine of an officer, which I would have learned through some form of orientation or on-the-job-training.

Fortunately, the inmate once lived on a block behind our childhood home, and we attended grammar school together. When I reflect on what had happened, it reminds me of the Golden Rule; it is always nice to meet someone from the good old days who is not nursing any grudge against you. I later thanked him, and although, he never asked for favors, he simply requested an extra dinner tray. That experience taught me how to respect not only the staff, but also the inmates as well.

It is interesting to note how smart the inmates were; most of them were well-versed in the practice of the correctional facility, which could also be used against a naive officer. Indeed, my encounter with my old school mate was a blessing that possibly saved the day and my career; however, that experience was also a wake-up call for officers and managers of correctional institutions, as I discovered how lax the security was.

There is a saying: "If the keel of a ship is damaged, there is a strong possibility that the ship will sink." When we consider the correctional facility as the ship, several questions start to emerge. Is it sinking? Is there a mutiny? Are there pirates on board? Did the captain of the ship jump overboard? If these metaphors sound familiar, then it is time for a review of the practices at our correctional facilities before it is too late. Prevention has always been better than a cure, and a certain way to stay afloat is to design and manage an accredited correctional facility with great leadership.

"The single biggest way to impact an organization is to focus on leadership development. There is almost no limit to the potential of an organization that recruits good people, raises them up as leaders and continually develops them." John C Maxwell: The 17th Irrefutable Laws of Teamwork (2001, 185)

Every stakeholder in the administration of the correctional facility needs to continually develop their potential, the staff must be brave, well-trained, and competent, and they should be ready to deal with wide-ranging challenges throughout their career. Effective leadership requires every officer to be ready to think outside the box while also honoring the Golden Rule, which is the source of fairness and justice to humanity. The quality of training and mentorship that officers get will determine the effectiveness of their leadership abilities. This will also impact the overall success of correctional institutions in fulfilling their mandate of ensuring the safety and security of inmates and officers, as well as society.

Despite the fact that I started out on a sinking ship, I was not ready to jump ship or drown; rather, I learned all I could to keep the ship afloat, and when I retired, my ship was floating on an even keel! The success of every correctional agency greatly depends on well-thought-out plans; effective plans and guidelines ensure that the facility functions seamlessly. The tools in this book will help every leader and staff of correctional agencies and law enforcement services to solve the most daunting challenges they face daily in the execution of their jobs.

I am delighted to share my experiences while I was in service to help you master some of the biggest challenges that I discovered during my career that will help you become a game changer in your profession. The challenges facing the correctional institutions have been on the increase, ranging from security and safety of both the inmates and the staff to the rehabilitation of inmates in order to ensure a safer and better community when the inmates leave the correctional facility.

The challenges that correctional institutions face have been on the increase, and one of the biggest challenges facing correctional institutions is mental health. It is a fact from available statistics that a large number of inmates in correctional institutions have mental health issues. According to a special report from the Bureau of Justice Statistics in 2005, more than half of jail inmates had mental health problems. How do correctional officers deal with such an increasing number of mentally ill inmates?

There are also increasing cases of violence in correctional institutions, such as inmate-to-inmate violence and staff assault. How can correctional officers effectively deal with offenses related to violence, which include rape and sexual assault? Most inmates are well-versed in correction matters, which increases the likelihood of lawsuits against officers and agencies that are not knowledgeable about such guidelines and procedures in corrections. How can officers reduce the rate of lawsuits against officers and agencies? Managers of correctional agencies need to know how to effectively prepare for emergencies that could occur anytime to ensure the safety of inmates, officers, and the society. What is the basic information needed in emergency preparedness of correctional institutions?

Safer Jail and Prison Matters provides you with effective answers to these challenging questions that correctional officers face daily. It provides distilled information that is designed to assist correctional officers and agencies in improving their leadership and management skills, prevent inmate violence and several correctional issues that plague our correctional system today. The level of information that we have usually determines the extent of our efficiency in dealing with everyday issues in our lives, and in our profession.

CHAPTER ONE
Effective Leadership and Management Practices

Introduction

Despite the fact that most departments in correctional facilities organize rigorous academic training for employees and officers, there is less emphasis placed on leadership development. Virtually all levels of managers will benefit from increased focus on leadership development. Blanding (2008) stated that one of the most often cited reasons employees leave an organization in exit surveys is usually their relationship with their supervisor.

> *"One of the most critical challenges facing criminal justice professionals today and in the future is the availability, recruitment, and retention of a qualified, diverse workforce"*
>
> *(Boyer D. K, 2004).*

This implies that the problem can easily be avoided or greatly reduced with good leadership. Developing effective leadership and management skills should, therefore, be one of the major focuses of correctional organizations.

Definition of Leadership

There have been arguments in the academic community regarding a precise definition of leadership; however, the late Peter Drucker noted that the only definition of a leader is someone who has followers. Building on this definition, Shaun Killian (2007) defines it as:

> *...any behavior that influences the actions and attitudes of followers to achieve certain results.*

Effective leadership in an organization should possess the following qualities:

- The ability of the management of an organization to make very good decisions and inspire others to perform very well.
- An organization with effective leadership should be able to set challenging goals and also achieve the goals.
- They should also be able to take swift and decisive action, even when they encounter difficult situations.
- Effective leadership should also be able to take calculated risks and endure, even when failure seems inevitable.
- Effective leadership should have the resources to outperform their competition.

Leadership Styles

Leadership styles can best be described as a leader's way of providing direction, motivating people and implementing plans. There are several leadership styles, and different situations will require different leadership styles. Blake and Mouton (1964) rendered five basic leadership styles based on concern for production and people. They include:

- **Country club management** - Which provides maximum concern for people and minimum concern for production.
- **Team management** - The leader is concerned with the people and productivity.
- **Authority-compliance** - Leaders using this style of leadership place focus on maximizing production and having less concern for people.
- **Impoverished management** - The leader executes minimum work that is needed to be a member of the organization.
- **Middle-of-the-road management** - Leaders do not conform to the status quo or make waves, despite the fact that they do their job.

Power and Leadership

The level of power you have determines the extent of your capacity to influence others, including employees in your organization. There are five potential sources of power:

- Interpersonal power
- Positional Power
- Expertise
- Reward Power (the carrot)
- Coercive Power (the stick)

Leadership in Correctional Organizations

Considering the depleting government budgets, correctional organizations need to operate effectively and efficiently, and this is possible with effective leadership. Leadership is a crucial factor in contemporary corrections as a result of several factors which affect correctional organizations, such as budget cutbacks, high turnover rates, legal mandates, rapidly increasing incarceration rates, technological mandates and other factors.

Apart from managing these changes, effective leadership and management is essential to help lead the staff members of correctional organizations.

"The quality of prison life depends far more on management practices than on any other single variable...if most prisons have failed, it is because they have been ill-managed, under-managed or not managed at all" (Dilulio, 1987).

While it is common for leaders to identify what is universal among their employees and then mobilize their employees towards achieving set goals, great managers rather discover, develop and celebrate the differences in each employee and integrate their uniqueness into the work plan (Buckingham, 2005).

Improving Employee Morale

Effective leadership and management will require great managers to engage employees, and in order to effectively do so, it is necessary to first understand what is important to the employees in order for them to be effective in their roles. This observation is based on the result from a national survey data obtained from Gallup Organization (2002). One of the least expensive ways of achieving organizational success is for managers to carry out a survey of staff and act on the results of the survey. Kimball and Nink (2006) stated that using this method will ensure that managers focus more on developing employees around their strengths. Employees will function better when they are assigned to duties and responsibility they have the necessary skills to execute, and when they successfully carry out their work, their confidence level increases.

Core Competencies of Correctional Leaders

Leaders should be able to guide the thoughts and actions of their followers by using their power. Despite the fact that most followers do not want to be led, good leaders should understand this; however, correctional system's leadership requires more than just power, listening and relating to others, they should be able to protect, create, take risks, question the status quo, stimulate growth and change and maintain routines (Williamsburg VA: Author 2003).

Charismatic leadership is gradually becoming scarce, and this extends to correctional organizations. There is a need for new forms of leadership with competencies that will provide effective leadership. You will find the ten correctional leaders competencies by (Montgomery M. J, 2006) useful.

Focus on the Big Picture

Correctional management should have a clear vision for the organization, and emphasis should be placed on the important things. This function is a primary determinant of the effectiveness of a leader, "creating a vision of the future that already exists in the mind of others" (Denhardt, 2004).

Identify Areas of Responsibility

Effective leaders should be able to frequently observe their areas of responsibility. Most times, correctional leaders believe that they have so much to do in office and then delegate the inspection of internal operations to staff, and this move has always ended in disaster; leaders are held responsible when there is a crisis.

Handle and Resolve Problems Quickly

The staff of correctional facilities is aware of pending problems, and if proper attention is not given to the problems, they assume that the leadership could not care less about them. The leaders should be able to carefully listen and understand existing problems, identify the areas of responsibility, develop effective strategies that will enable them to solve the problems, implement a plan for the resolution of any problems and be ready to evaluate and alter the plan if necessary.

Effectively Attend to All Inquiries

Correctional organization leaders get many inquiries daily, and they should be responsive to all inquiries, both internal and external. By their nature, correctional systems have a complex structure and are therefore inaccessible to the public; however, (Clear, 1999) argued that U.S. prisons need to be accessible in order to enable the citizens understand how they work.

Effective Communication

They communicate with individuals both internal and external to the correctional organization by clearly stating their values and vision to staff, volunteers, and other organizations. A great trait of effective leaders is the ability to convey sincerity and dedication to the missions of the organization so that citizens and followers can willingly choose to align to that purpose. One of the effective elements of effective communication is listening. (Denhardt, 2004) stated the importance of leaders to practice empathetic listening.

Constantly Enhance Their Abilities

By enhancing their abilities, leaders should learn about their organizations, themselves, followers and industry. This can be achieved by constant reading of books, attending seminars and conferences and exchange of ideas.

Effective Leaders Should Nurture Their Staff

Effective leaders should appreciate their employees, assign responsibilities to them and make efforts to retain them. Most individuals in the United States are mainly interested in business (Kiel, 2003); therefore, those who desire to work in public service should be nurtured and encouraged.

Integrate Integrity as a Core Value

The citizenry has high expectations of public office holders, and correctional leaders are not exempted; rather, a higher level of integrity is needed from them, as integrity is everything in correctional leadership. (Stohr, et al. 2000) argued that in corrections specifically, the right choice is easily understood and can be executed, though it may not be the easiest line of action to take. The correctional leader should be able to create a platform where employees will strive to do the right thing. The leader can achieve this by being a great example, disciplining those who default from acceptable norms fairly and rewarding or acknowledging those who exhibit extraordinary ethical behavior.

Solve Problems With Their Skills

Effective correctional leaders should be ready to offer their skills towards solving problems in their organization. When they do this, they set examples for the employees to also do the same.

Think Outside The Box, And Yet Be Reasonable

Correctional leaders must be creative and innovative in order to meet the needs of the ever-changing system and society. Staff should also be encouraged to provide their ideas freely to aid in resolving organizational problems.

Habits Of Highly Effective People

"We are what we repeatedly do."

Aristotle

Our habits constantly express our character. Our habits are consistent, and that is why habits produce our effectiveness or ineffectiveness. Effective leadership is a habit that every leader should cultivate, because excellence is not an act, but a habit. There are habits that are shared by effective people, and according to (Steven R. Covey, 2004), there are seven habits of highly effective people:

- **Proactivity** - Rather than being reactive, we have to take responsibility for our lives. Identify your responsibility, take action and make things happen. Do whatever it takes, based on the right principles to get the best results.
- **Begin With The End In Mind** - Effective leaders know where they are going, and you should have in mind what you intend to achieve. Have a personal mission statement which will describe what you want to achieve and who you want to be.

- **Put First Things First** - Learn to prioritize, know what comes first and develop the discipline to do the first things before others. For you to be a good manager of yourself, you need to organize and execute your goals based on your priorities.
- **Seek to Understand, Then Be Understood** - Effective leadership requires that you learn to listen to others, see things from their perspective and understand them. You need to develop the skill of empathy, because it provides you with accurate data or feedback from your colleagues to work with. This is a better approach than imposing your motives and thoughts on them.
- **Think Win/Win** - Effective leaders should learn to allow all parties involved to benefit from a decision or an action. This is a long-term benefit and can be achieved through self-discipline, which is a foundation for a good relationship with other people. A win/win habit requires: integrity, maturity, and an abundance mentality.
- **Synergize** - The practice of other habits prepares you for the habit of synergy, the ability to value and exploit the emotional, mental and psychological differences between people.
- **Sharpen the Saw** - By sharpening your saw, you need to renew yourself in four aspects of life: physical, mental, social/emotional and spiritual.

The Laws of Success

There are several laws of success that will ensure absolute success for every leader. They are actually qualities of great leadership. The 16 laws of success, by Napoleon Hill, is summarized below:

- **You Need to Know Your Definite Major Aim** - Set a goal and aim for the goal, you will definitely achieve it.
- **Imbibe the Principle of the Mastermind** - It relates to telepathy, vibration, ether and how they all function in our world. Mastermind relates to the power achieved when two or more minds come together in unity.
- **Develop Self-Confidence** - Have a strong belief that you deserve success and that you can attain it.
- **Learn to Save** - Learn to save from every money you get, you accumulate wealth gradually.

- **Be an Enthusiast** - Combine enthusiasm with your work, you will not get tired easily.
- **Build your Imagination** - Use your imagination, dream and take action.
- **Leadership and Initiative** - Develop leadership skills, and you will attain success.
- **Do More Than You Are Paid For** - You will make yourself an asset, rather than a liability.
- **Learn The habit of Self Control** - Replace your old beliefs with positive and new ones that will serve you better.
- **Develop Accurate Thoughts** - Learn to differentiate between facts and information.
- **Have a Pleasant Personality** - To be successful, you have to be pleasant.
- **Foster Cooperation** - By cooperating with other people, you build a network of people for success.
- **Learn to Concentrate** - By focusing on specific desires, you achieve them faster.
- **Imbibe the Golden Rule** - Learn to do to others what you would like them to do to you.
- **Be Tolerant** - Always see the best in other people.
- **Learn From Failure** - Every failure brings you closer to your success, it is an opportunity to do better.

Effective leadership is the foundation of successful organizations, their duties, and responsibilities, when handled, will ensure that organizational goals are achieved. There should be effective communication between the leader and the followers. When a leader effectively communicates the vision and goals of the organization to everyone, corporate goals are easily achieved faster. Leaders should constantly imbibe the habit of personal development and also learn to develop the skills and talents of their followers. When employees are trained and empowered for leadership roles, they will be able to handle responsibilities which will allow them to delegate duties where needed.

Summary

Considering the increasing number of diversity of inmates in the nation's prisons, the complexity of the political, social and legal climate that we operate presently and the challenging responsibilities that have been placed on correctional organizations and agencies, it has become very important for correctional organizations and agencies to clearly identify and train effective leaders at all levels of management in the organization.

This includes the frontline supervisors and heads of correctional institutions, and the starting point is to identify the skills and attributes of an effective correctional leader, which is their core competencies, and then seek ways and avenues that the skills can be developed. One of the foundations of good management and supervision is the ethical behavior of leaders. Every democratic society where individual human dignity and excellence in performance are valued, competence, accountability and ethics based on respect are critical, and this is true for correctional institutions, because they have access to the use of force and coercion (Campbell, 2006).

Correctional supervisors and managers should be aware of the threats to ethics in the institution, which include: denial of responsibility, peer culture, tensions that are created by diversity, such as differences in ethnic and racial makeup between correction officers and inmates, the silence or secrecy concerning discrimination, ethical lapses and abuse and dominant informal actors, which include individuals that have excessive influence in a correctional institution due to their knowledge of the operations of the institution, experience or their ability to grant favors.

Some of the key competencies of effective leaders in correctional institutions, which include supervisors and managers, include:

- The ability to manage conflict
- Team building
- Decision-making abilities
- A good interpersonal relationship skill
- Problem-solving
- Strategic thinking
- Knowledge of the criminal justice system
- Program planning and performance assessment
- Ability to motivate others
- Collaboration

One of the core competencies that managers and supervisors in correctional institutions should develop is effective communication.

As soon as you move one step up from the bottom, your effectiveness depends on your ability to reach others through the spoken or written word.

(Peter F. Drucker, Father of Modern Management)

Communication is a two-way process that enables ideas and feelings to be expressed by the sender of a message which the receiver gets and understands clearly. Leaders should be able to effectively communicate the visions and goals of the institution to all staff, and they should also encourage effective communication among staff (Campbell, 2006).

Helping all stakeholders to understand the value of the correctional institution's service is one of the critical tasks of leaders and executives in correctional institutions. Leaders should be able to create a vision capable of capturing the hearts and the imagination of prison officers, inmates, people in the community and other stakeholders. The vision should help correction officers to understand the value of their calling, which is to serve the community or the public that most times, condemn and rejects corrections' clients, which happen to be inmates, and also the inmates who also condemn and reject their circumstances (Campbell, 2005).

A vision is a target that beckons.

(Bennis et al. 1985)

Every great leader should periodically take stock of his personal shortcomings and strengths and hire people to complement him in his areas of weakness. They are responsive to the needs of their teams, which requires good perception. Effective leaders should also have a good understanding of the organization where they work, and this includes the purpose and goals and the strategies that have been accepted for dealing with complex organizational issues (University Alliance).

"You need the humility to remind yourself that you've got to get better at everything you do," insisted Amazon founder Jeff Bezos. "I don't know about you, but I'm never done growing my company or myself."

The National Institute of Corrections, American Corrections Association (ACA) and the American Jail Association (AJA) are some of the organizations that provide training and certification opportunities which will help correction officers develop their leadership skills and also rise in their career. Leaders should always strive to develop, because there is always room for improvement.

Keywords: Correctional Organization, Leadership, Management, Employees, Power, Corrections, Habits, Staff, Success, Goals, Justice, Employee, Develop.

CHAPTER TWO

The Effective Use of Force

The use of force continuum is a standard which provides guidelines for law enforcement officers and civilians on how much force may be applied against a resisting subject, which could be an inmate or a suspect in any given situation. One of the most common reasons inmates file a lawsuit against correction officers or correctional facilities is the way and manner in which force was used on the inmate.

Corrections officers need to know the prison rule 47 YOI rule 50:

"An officer in dealing with a prisoner shall not use force unnecessarily, and when the application of force is necessary, no more force than is necessary shall be used."

They should be conscious of this rule in dealing with inmates. Officers must make all reasonable effort to control disturbed and violent inmates, and the use of force should be the last resort. The definition of violence for correctional facilities is:

"...any incident in which a person is abused, threatened or assaulted. This includes an explicit or implicit challenge to their safety, well-being or health. The resulting harm may be physical, emotional or psychological."

(The Use of Force Training Manual, 2006)

There is a possibility of litigation any time corrections officers use force on an inmate, and the corrections staff should be well-informed about the continuum of force, because it could result in a lawsuit where it was not properly applied. Corrections officers should ensure that videos of their encounters with inmates when the use of force was applied are preserved, and they should be reviewed by command staff and supervisors.

Types of Force Techniques

There are different types of force technique that officers can use in dealing with inmates, and the one to be applied depends on the situation. Some of the force techniques include:

- **Personal Safety** - This type of force is used appropriately in order to prevent the inmate from harming the officer or other people.
- **Batons** - The use of batons is for defensive purposes in extreme circumstances, provided the officers are aware of the relevant medical implications.
- **Control and Restrain** - This type of force is used as a last resort to control a violent or refractory inmate, and it is to be applied within a short time.

The use of force can be regarded as lawful when its use meets certain requirements.

Factors to Consider Before the Use of Force

Before the use of force is applied by officers, there are certain factors they need to consider; they are officer factors and inmate factors.

- **Inmate Factors** - The following inmate factors need to be considered by corrections officers before the use of force:
    - The size, weight and age of inmate
    - The nature of offense or violation
    - Is the offender armed?
    - The number of prisoners involved needs to be considered
    - Does the offender has a history of violence?
    - The physical ability of the inmate also needs to be considered
    - Is the inmate resisting or submitting?

- Officers need to assess the level of support from other officers before the use of force

- **Officer Factors** - Officers need to also consider factors that have to do with them and their colleagues, such as:
    - The weapons and restraint devices that are available to the officer
    - The policy of the correctional facility
    - The legal requirements
    - The physical ability, size and the defensive tactics level of the officer
    - The number of officers that are available

Prison officers should be ready at all times, based on experience and training, so as to respond immediately to violent acts by inmates that have little to no regard for life (Flesch, 1994).

Corrections officers may be faced with circumstances where they need to use force to control a violent or unreasonable inmate; however, the officers involved in the use of force are accountable for their actions. The status or orders received cannot be used as a justification for the use of force. When force is used by an officer, the following information needs to be recorded:

- All the correction officers must record what led to the use of force
- They must state the reasons for the level of force that was used
- All information that is relevant regarding the circumstances should also be recorded

The Use of Force in Correctional Facilities

The use of force by one individual on another without permission is unlawful unless it is justified, and it will be justified based on the following conditions:

- The use of force will be justified if it is necessary
- Force can be used if it is proportionate to the level of seriousness of the incident
- Force can be used if no more force than is required is used
- The use of force will be justified provided it is reasonable in the circumstances

Reasonable In the Circumstances

One of the major issues regarding the use of force in correctional facilities is the interpretation of reasonable, and the issue of the reasonableness of the force is a matter of fact to be decided in individual cases. The circumstances are usually different and unique and will be judged based on the merits of the facts. Some factors that will be considered when deliberating on what is reasonable include things like sex, age, the size of the inmate and the correctional staff involved in the case of the use of force. The use of a weapon will also be considered (PSO 1600, 2015).

Necessary Force

Before corrections officers use force, such action must have been necessary. It is much easier to interpret the use of force in "self-defense" as a necessary force, rather than the use of force on an inmate when a lawful order was not obeyed. Another point to consider when dealing with the use of force is the level of harm that the staff is trying to avoid; such considerations will help to determine if the use of force is necessary, based on the circumstances they encountered. The following risks can be regarded as harm:

- Risk to property
- Risk to life
- Risk to limb
- Risk to the great order of the facility

The use of force when the officer's limb or life is at risk is justifiable.

Use of Force and Medical Procedures

It is very important that officers who are involved in the use of force in correctional facilities need to know the signs and symptoms which show that an inmate is in medical distress. Inmates who show such signs will have to be treated as a medical emergency instead of a restraint and control incident. When a violent inmate is being restrained, the supervisor and officer involved need to watch out for signs like:

- Coughing or foaming from the mouth
- Labored breathing
- Sudden and abnormal passivity
- Legs, lips, face becoming purple or pale

- Unexpected or exceptional strength
- Abnormally high tolerance of pain
- Unusual rise in the body temperature of the inmate
- Exceptional violence
- Bizarre behavior (PSO 1600, 2015)

How to Subdue Inmates with the Use of Force

Most departments and correctional facilities educate their officers on how to escalate force, starting with:

- The presence of the officer
- The use of verbal command by the officer
- Using soft hand techniques
- The use of hard hand techniques, which will include pepper spray, or if authorized, Tasers can be used
- The use of DPF (deadly physical force) comes as a last resort (Osterstuck, 2012)

The Use of Force Options

The use of force options means the choices that are available to corrections officers when they are making a choice of the most reasonable force option when dealing with an inmate. There are several choices, and some of them include:

- Verbal persuasion or dialogue
- Mechanical restraints
- Physical strengths and holds
- Chemical restraints
- Less-lethal weapons
- Firearms

The use of less-lethal weapons refers to a corrections officer's use of a security device that has been approved by the department, and this includes the use of weapons that are used to fire less-lethal projectiles. Firearms refers to approved firearms, which include the weapons that are used to fire lethal projectiles (CDCR).

Procedural Justice and the Use of Force

The understanding of the individual's experience in dealing with legal authorities such as the corrections officers, police, and others is very important. Based on research, it has been discovered that legitimacy (regardless of the way it is defined) is associated with the fairness of the procedure that authorities exercise their authority (Tyler & Huo, 2002).

Based on the U.S. work on procedural justice, the major factor that shapes the individual's evaluation of the court and the police is the level of fairness of the manner in which authority was exercised - procedural justice (Tyler, 2007, 2008). This implies that the legitimate decisions of legal authorities should be made through fair procedures, which makes people more willing to accept the decisions voluntarily and adhere to them across time, even though their behavior is being monitored (Tyler and Huo, 2002).

The overall judgments regarding the level of fairness of authorities help to shape the people's compliance with the law, which also extends to the inmates, and it also influences their willingness to cooperate in an effort to maintain social order in the communities and the correctional facilities. There are four factors that affect the generation of procedural justice in correctional facilities: neutrality, voice, trust in authorities and treatment with respect and dignity (Jackson et al. 2010).

Voice

This implies giving inmates the chance to participate in the decision-making process. It creates an opportunity for them to state their case before major decisions are made by the staff of correctional facilities in situations that have to do with daily conflicts and disagreements. By allowing them to be part of the decision-making process, inmates are given the opportunity to express their personal concerns, their views about what issues are involved and also make suggestions on how such issues should be resolved (Tyler and Huo, 2002).

Neutrality

The concept of neutrality refers to decision making that is based on the consistent application of rules, which is based on proper procedure rather than on prejudices or personal opinions. The prison facility creates a considerable platform for the arbitrary and capricious exercise of power, and for the authorities to act based on prejudice and implicit bias; however, by acting based on rules, and also by the application of those rules evenly across inmates and time, the prison authority will be viewed by inmates as acting fairly. Considering the fact that the rules are explicitly specified in jail settings, the prison authorities possess a reasonable capacity to shape and provide explanations for their actions by making reference to the rules.

Treatment

Generally, inmates feel subjected to negative stereotypes. They regard themselves as diminished as humans and also feel disrespected beyond what is appropriate when dealing with the law. By acknowledging the inmate's rights and acting with courtesy, inmates feel fairly treated.

Trust in the Authority

When people feel that the authorities are acting based on a sincere desire to do the right thing, their perception of the authorities will be that they are acting more fairly, and when they view that the authority is not concerned about their well-being, inmates are bound to react negatively to the actions of the authority.

In a correctional facility where individuals from minority ethnic groups experience the loss of their privilege and the use of force, inmates will most likely interpret this as the failure of procedure, which is:

- The failure to treat them with dignity and fairness
- Failure for the authorities to be neutral in their treatment and decision-making
- The failure to be clear about what the rules are and to consistently apply them fairly

The use of force disproportionately or an increased use of segregation seems to communicate denial of voice, disrespect and the failure by corrections officers to wield authority in a fair, neutral and unbiased manner.

The fight over dominance can be defused by the interaction that is based on cooperation and fairness, and the most effective strategy for negotiation for both the inmates and the officers (though not always) is to start with cooperation, but to also respond to competition when the opponent reciprocates with competition. A procedural justice-based policing strategy similarly does not mean the use of force and should not be used when a hostile inmate is involved; rather, it means to the extent to which the officers can elicit compliance without the use of force (Axelrod, 1984).

CPI Training and De-escalation Techniques

The major factor in the de-escalation of crises is communication. There will most likely be a moment to make a quick assessment of a situation by corrections officers before stepping in. Based on CPI training on the prevention of violence and intervention in crises, the behavior of the inmate involved should be evaluated before taking action, if necessary. The importance of empathic listening is usually stressed when trying to understand where an inmate or an individual is coming from, and empathic listening can be learned (CPI, 2003). There are five keys to empathic listening:

Provide Undivided Attention

People feel important and validated when they are paid attention to, and the opposite is also true: inmates feel less important and have a feeling that they need to up the ante when they need attention. Paying attention is more than just listening; it involves looking at the person, listening to the entire body and where applicable, making eye contact, though not also the case in correctional facilities. This takes away the inmate's reason for escalating a situation (CPI, 2003).

Officers Should be NonJudgmental

Apart from paying attention to what people say, officers should also ensure that their tone and body language are non-judgmental, too.

Emphasize Feelings

By focusing on the feelings of the individual, it will elicit a positive response, because the individual will have an understanding that the officer knows what is happening.

Give Room for Silence

Sometimes, allowing silence is a great choice when dealing with individuals, especially when interrogating them. Silence provides the individual with the chance to think of an answer or hear properly. When an officer allows a moment of silence, the individual may show a sign of confusion on his/her face. By observing the confusion, the officer needs to repeat the question again for clarity. One good reason for the silence is that no one likes silence, and people will likely start talking when the silence is prolonged (CPI, 2003).

Clarify Messages

Sometimes statements or questions can be misinterpreted as a challenge by other people, and this makes the individual defensive. In situations like this, restatement is necessary. In CPI, the ability of an officer to exercise self-control when handling violent offenders is very important; it is a factor known as "rational detachment", which is a key factor that determines the possibility of an officer de-escalating or escalating the situation. In order to detach rationally:

- Officers need to develop a plan. The decisions that are made before crises occur have proven to be more rational than the decisions made when the officer is on the receiving end of emotional outbursts.
- Whenever possible, a team approach should be used, because professionalism is easily maintained when assistance is close.
- Use positive self-talk.
- There is a need to recognize personal limits. Being an officer does not mean that there are no limitations; rather, officers should know their limitations and sometimes allow others to take over.
- Officers should debrief with team members, co-workers or a supervisor after a major incident; it helps to relieve some of the stress and serves as a means to plan for future encounters (CPI, 2003).

Dealing with Mentally Ill Inmates

There are more mentally ill individuals in correctional institutions than in mental hospitals and therapeutic settings. This is mainly due to the deinstitutionalization of the mentally ill. The stress of imprisonment can further aggravate the mental illness symptoms if proper care is not taken. This makes life more difficult for the inmates while in correctional facilities. The Bureau of Justice reported that inmates with mental illness are more likely to violate prison rules and be involved in staff assaults and altercations than inmates without mental illness. Correction officers need to understand and manage mentally ill offenders to reduce the possibility of lawsuits and stress from such encounters. Here are some effective tips on how to handle mentally ill inmates (Schoenly, 2014).

Be Conscious of Mental Illness Early

It will be easy for corrections officers to assume that every non-conforming or aggressive behavior of inmates is an intentional act to break the rules (although much of such acts can be); however, officers need to have an early consciousness of the possibility of mental illness in a situation. Although, some settings may classify seriously mentally ill inmates, unclassified inmates may not have been diagnosed, or they may have a mild mental illness which is the cause of their behavior. When they are treated, it will lessen the potential for staff and inmate injuries.

Partner with Mental Health Professionals

Corrections officers need to leverage on mental health professionals, develop good relationships with psychologists, counselors, and psychiatrists, and get some help from them. They have the expertise to intervene in constructive ways in an encounter with mentally ill inmates that are escalating. They can come up with an ongoing treatment plan which includes structured responses to inmates' behaviors.

Mental Training

Correction officers can handle mentally ill inmate more effectively when they invest time in mental health training. There are many mental health resources available, and the more officers know about mental illness, the easier it will be for them to detect and respond properly and successfully to issues with mentally ill inmates. Some correctional facilities provide basic mental health training for front-line staff and officers as part of ongoing professional development and orientation. Officers can also obtain additional training on how to deal with mentally ill inmates by persuading mental health staff to assist with case presentation and debriefing of real situations in the correctional facility.

Request for Medical Evaluation

There are several psychiatric manifestations that originate from medical conditions; for instance, electrolyte imbalance or liver disease can result in symptoms of mental illness, like paranoia, depression, and moodiness. It will be proper to carry out a medical evaluation, and a mental health consult will be a great strategy, especially for inmates that developed unexpected changes in their thinking and behavior (Schoenly, 2014).

Tips on How to Deal with Mentally Ill Inmates

The following tips will be very useful to correction officers when dealing with mentally ill inmates:

- Officers should request for backup corrections officers when taking the inmate into custody.
- Take steps to calm the inmate, and if possible, remove sirens, emergency lights and disperse any crowds. Let the location be non-threatening and quiet, and if there is no physical contact, avoid it.
- Do not excite the disturbed inmate; move slowly and provide assurance that officers are there to help out.
- Engage in communication in a bid to determine what is bothering the inmate; allow the inmates to ventilate their feelings.
- Avoid threatening the inmate with arrests or other forms of threat that will create extra fright or potential aggression.
- Stay away from topics that may agitate the inmate, and guide the inmate towards subjects that will lead the inmate to reality.
- Be as truthful as possible; when mentally ill inmates detect deception, they may withdraw from the contact due to distrust and may retaliate in anger (Jack Ryan).

The circumstances in which officers need to control inmates with the use of force differs, and there is a need for discretion and a great understanding of the policies and procedures regarding the use of force. All the information regarding the incident needs to be documented to help the officers defend their actions in the event of a lawsuit. The use of force should only be used when all other methods of dispute resolution have been exhausted, and there should be fairness in the use of force by officers.

Summary

The use of force must only be applied when all other options available to the corrections officer have been exhausted or when those options are not appropriate; for instance, in a life threatening situation. The need for the use of force can be avoided in certain circumstances: when there are frequent patrols by correctional officers, the presence and the instruction of senior officers and when there is persuasion and negotiation with inmates (Ombudsman NSW, 2012).

The minimum amount of force necessary in any situation should only be used by correctional officers, and the level of force must be reasonable and appropriate in the circumstances. It is important to note that once an inmate has been restrained satisfactorily, no extra force needs to be applied except the force that is needed to maintain the restraint, and the application of force must be stopped if it is no longer necessary to restrain the inmate, because the application of force beyond this point is unlawful (Ministry of Justice, 2006).

The use of force is a tactic of last resort, and it must only be used when there are no other alternatives. The level of force applied must be appropriate, reasonable and it must be the minimum necessary in the circumstances. When force is no longer needed to control the circumstances or inmates, it must be stopped. A planned use of force provides the correctional officers with sufficient time for assessing the situation if there are alternatives to the use of force, and if the use of force is unavoidable, what type of force should be used (Ombudsman NSW, 2012).

A camera must be available when there is a planned use of force; it will be used to record the conversations and actions of all those involved, which includes the inmates and the officers. It is also important that officers that use force and those who witnessed the use of force should write an independent incident report which contains the following information: the date and time that force was used, the location, identities of all those involved, detailed information describing the conversation or statements made and those who made the statement, the nature of the force that was applied and other relevant information (Ombudsman NSW, 2012).

New recruits need to be trained concerning the use of force; this will train recruits on the appropriate response in any given situation. Recruits should be trained in defensive tactics such as palm strikes, stances, kicks and stepping, which should only be used when the circumstances are reasonable and necessary. Other areas of training for students include the use of chemical agents, batons and weapon handling. At the end of the training, the recruits are tested on physical restraint skills.

Although correctional officers have been trained on the use of force before they started working in correctional facilities, such training might have been done several years ago. There is a need for an ongoing training that will serve as a refresher course and to educate officers of the significant changes that might have occurred since their last training.

Keywords: Procedural justice, Use of force, Lawsuit, Litigation, De-escalation, Defuse, Violent, Inmate, Correctional facility.

CHAPTER THREE

Effective Methods to Prevent and Reduce Inmate Violence

It is a common perception that correctional facilities are dangerous due to the fact that they house violent inmates and criminals. The union representing prison officers in California, for example, emphasized the danger associated with the job by calling it "the toughest beat in the state". In 2013, about 11,000 cases of assaults by inmates on other inmates were recorded, and the rate of serious assaults increased by 14 percent between 2010 and 2013 (Prison Reform Trust, 2014). Corrections officers prevent hundreds of assaults and fights daily, and this is usually achieved when they notice signs of tension and trouble and know when to intervene properly.

The success of the goal of making correctional facilities less violent can only be achieved if the correction officers are able to execute their jobs with accountability, consistency, and professionalism. They need to fully understand the importance of safe prisons, which positively affects the inmates, prison staff, and the community.

One major reason why staff interventions and violence reduction strategies are not very effective in the reduction of violence in correctional facilities is because of the lack of information regarding the circumstances which caused the violence. Most times, the information gathered regarding inmate violence is obtained from prison officers that responded to the problem after the violence has erupted. This makes the cause or root of the problem difficult to understand, especially in prisons where inmates may not freely disclose such information.

Why Violence?

Understanding the motivation behind inmates' violence is a useful tool in preventing violence in correctional facilities. What motivates the use of violence by inmates? Based on the results of a research by (Edgar et al. 2003), the following factors were associated with violence in prisons:

- Drugs were involved in several violent incidents. One in ten incidents recorded the issue of drugs, and this was slightly more among women inmates.
- The beating of a suspected informant or suspected cell thief is the cause of a third of assaults and fights in prisons.
- About a quarter of violent incidents involve inmates who through the use of violence want to project a tough image to other inmates who are not involved in the dispute.
- Also, a quarter of violent incidents involves inmates who use force when they are faced with an imminent threat to their safety.

Other factors that have been associated with higher levels of violence in correctional facilities include:

- The quality and experience of the corrections officers
- Prison crowding, ineffective inmate classification practices
- Inadequate programming in corrections facilities
- Poor management practices
- Inadequate prison design

(Byrne et al. 2005)

Power Contests Among Inmates

"Prison life is characterized by ongoing negotiations of power."

(Bosworth, M and Carrabine E, 2001)

There is a widespread concern regarding intimidation in correctional facilities, and the most frequent situations leading to violence are power contests. When inmates get involved in a fight over little issues, like access to the pool table or some material object, the inmates are likely to defend their self-respect and honor. Some of the features of power contests among inmates include:

- **Respect** - The central concern is usually being dominated
- **Sizing up** - There is also the measurement of the opponent's strength of character
- **Win/lose** - In correctional facilities, compromise is regarded as a weakness
- **Narrow focus** - There is usually focus on one's opponent/inmate
- **Power values** - The use of force determines the outcome of the contest
- **Precedent** - The loss of a dispute places the inmate concerned in an inferior position

Response Strategies to Prison Violence

Three broad categories of response to disorder and violence in correctional facilities are available:

- **Inmate-focused Strategies** - This strategy is designed to help resolve conflicts among prisoners by using conflict resolution techniques and restorative justice
- **Management-focused strategies** - It was designed to change the situational context of correctional facilities, in a bid to reduce disorder and violence in prisons. Management-centered strategies focus on a specific number of very promising situational prison control methods, such as:
    - The size of the correctional facility
    - Physical changes in the environment
    - Staffing characteristics
    - Staffing level
    - The protection of vulnerable inmates
    - Sanctioning practices
    - Program/treatment availability
- **Staff-focused strategies** - Focus is placed on changing the negative staff culture that exists in many correctional facilities, especially in the United States.

Considering New Safety Interventions

Before considering any new safety interventions in correctional facilities, the management of correctional facilities need to rely on a four-step process:

- They need to analyze the times, dates, locations and contexts that surround previous violent incidents in order to be able to take note of the factors that are related to the violence.
- There is a need for the application of evidence-based strategies to deal with the facility's vulnerabilities and specific needs.
- The strategies should be placed in an overall system of best practice for supervising, classifying and managing inmate, and designing prisons.
- The intervention should be evaluated continuously, and changes should be done where needed.

Effective Strategies to Reduce Violence in Prisons

According to (La Vigne, et al. 2011), most of the strategies explained here are current sound practices in different correctional facilities. These strategies offer insights that will aid the identification of underlying causes of violence in prisons and help to develop ways to deal with them.

The Need for Targeted Interventions

Due to the fact that the contextual factors, causes and opportunities to commit violent activities in correctional facilities may differ by the type of population or the type of violence, there is a need for targeted interventions to ensure that effective strategies aimed at reducing violence in correctional facilities are properly executed.

Proper Surveillance of Cells

Inmates actually acknowledge that cells are the high-risk location for contraband and violence, and the reason for this trend is that cells are not under any constant surveillance or supervision. The privacy requirements place a restriction on fixing cameras in cells; however, cameras can be strategically positioned to keep a record of all movements in and out of the cell when inmates are in the dayrooms.

There should also be an increased surveillance accountability in order to deter violence, and surveillance cameras should be strategically installed in areas that are termed "blind spots". These blind spots are areas that have been identified as high-risk areas where suicide and violent activities thrive.

When there is surveillance accountability, the data recorded will be used for investigation into the cause of the violence, and it will be much easier to resolve such conflicts. Although some corrections officers perceive the camera as a tool used to monitor their activities, jail administrators and inmates feel the use of a camera fosters a safer prison facility (La Vigne, et al. 2011).

Violence, Sex and Sexual Assault

Regarding the problem of sexual assault, it is evident that sexual violence and physical violence are usually interconnected. Consequently, jail administrators need to enforce a zero tolerance policy concerning consensual sex between prisoners and staff sexual misconduct. Basically, both cases are potential triggers for violence and also cover more serious sexual force in correctional facilities. The presence of officers should also be increased through direct supervision or increase in rounds to enhance the safety of the cells.

Access to Medical Care

The prisoner's inability to obtain mental health care or medicine in correctional facilities is a major trigger for inmate violence, and also self-harm. The quality of health care in correctional facilities should be improved, and inmates should have better access to health care in prison facilities.

Officers' Role In The Prevention of Violence

Conflict resolution in correctional facilities is far more effective in prisons when corrections officers challenge the harmful behavior of inmates who usually escalate, than react to violence with force after they occur. When prison staff confronts victimization consistently, it removes the causes of prison violence and increases the confidence of inmates that their conflicts can be resolved without violence. Corrections officers' roles can be summarized in three ways:

- They need to intervene in conflicts early and manage the dispute among inmates by placing focus on the values, interests and the inmate's needs at stake.
- They should strive to improve the communication between the parties.

- Finally, corrections officers should seek options that will provide a win-win outcome (Edgar, 2014).

The Role of Inmates

In order to ensure safer correctional facilities, inmates need to be consulted on ways to achieve a safer prison environment. This process of consulting them will provide prison administrators with vital information regarding the causes of the violent incidents, the resources among inmates that will help to prevent violence and an effective approach in managing the conflicts. Correctional facilities that create wing forums, impartial and trained mediators and formal avenues to negotiate have the right resources to resolve fights and conflicts in prisons effectively (Edgar, 2014).

The Role of Managers

Correctional facilities continually experience conflicts on a daily basis. The conflicts could be between staff and inmates, managers and staff and among inmates. Managers in correctional agencies need to develop a strategy that will help in resolving conflicts constructively. They should promote social order by promoting the objectives that address the major causes of conflict. These objectives include:

- Meeting the basic human needs of the inmates.
- Making provision for opportunities to exercise personal autonomy.
- Establishing mechanisms that will help prisoners to resolve their conflicts (Edgar, 2014).

Staff Training and Violence

Correction officers can effectively handle inmates and spot impending violence before it escalates; however, they need to be well-trained to handle conflicts and crisis intervention. Officers should be educated about sexual assault, suicide, and mental illness; these are usually major factors that lead to violence in correctional facilities.

Corrections officers' interaction with inmates will also help to reduce the frustration and stress that inmates experience while being incarcerated; this will lead to a great reduction in the level of confrontations that usually lead to provocation. Prison staff should be taught how to intervene and resolve intense situations without the use of violence. Corrections staff should also be trained to identify inmates with symptoms of sexual victimization, self-harm and mental illness (La Vigne, et al. 2011).

Consistent Inmates Supervision

When the supervision of inmates by corrections officers is inconsistent, inmates will be provided with the opportunity to engage in violent activities and confrontations. Corrections facilities should provide a better platform for consistent supervision of inmates, and the installation of sensor buttons in specific locations to help track officers' rounds with the device carried by officers will help to ensure that officers are held accountable (La Vigne, et al. 2011).

Prison Violence Prevention Tips

Strategic actions that corrections officers and jail administrators should take to ensure safer prisons with less violence are summarized with the following tips:

- The risk assessments should be updated regularly, and they should be based on dynamic factors.
- Officers should be alert to all forms of aggressive behavior.
- A dynamic security system provides prison staff with the resources for identifying signs of trouble early.
- There should be frequent wing meetings to discuss the causes of tension.
- The basic human needs of prisoners should be met.
- Correctional officers should learn to handle ethnic and racial tension.
- Corrections officers should be trained to effectively respond to conflicts.
- Inmates should be involved in the quest to reduce prison violence.
- There should be a strong enforcement of rules prohibiting weapons, drugs and other contraband in prisons.
- Jail administrators should reward non-violent response to conflicts.
- Good relationships should be fostered in correctional facilities.
- A regular correctional facility survey about inmate victimization will provide information regarding the factors that contribute to inmate violence (Edgar, 2014).

The purpose of correctional facilities is to help in the rehabilitation of inmates, as well as to provide a conducive environment where inmates can be rehabilitated. The safety of correctional facilities is essential in order to provide a humane penal system. It is a complex challenge to reduce violence in prisons; however, understanding conflicts provides insight into the underlying causes of assaults and fights and provides effective and dynamic tools for managing correctional facilities.

Summary

Several factors have been found to be associated with the increase in prison violence. Some of them include pre-existing prisoner characteristics, such as the inmate's age and gender, situational factors such as the architectural design and the level of security of the prison, and also management practices which could be prison officers' skills and training, staffing models and prison culture and management style. There are also external factors which are outside the prison environment, which include racial tensions and political pressures on prison administrators.

It is quite easy to blame inmates for the violence in prisons; however, the lessons from the last few decades of academic research and court intervention have demonstrated that the level of violence in correctional facilities is a function of its culture.

The poor management of prisons leading to dysfunctional forms of control is also a major cause of interpersonal violence, and this implies that the modification of these practices in prisons, especially the removal of arbitrary coercive controls, will be very effective in the reduction of prison violence. There are several effective strategies that will help to reduce the rate of inmate violence, and these strategies include the manipulation of prisoner privileges, improved surveillance of high-risk locations and an improved supervision of both inmates and corrections officers (Homel, et al. 2005).

There has been an increase in empirical research to support the use of situational strategies for reducing the level of prisoner-to-prisoner violence and other forms of prison violence, and some of the strategies include:

- Increasing inmates' control over their environment in order to encourage compliance and reduce frustration.
- Increase in women corrections officers may help encourage compliance and reduce frustration, which reduces assault on officers.
- The elimination of blind spots, which may improve formal and natural surveillance.
- Having age-heterogeneous prison population can reduce inappropriate imitation and conformity.

- The use of single-cell accommodation, which can reduce crowding and respect the inmate's territory while "target hardening" an inmate. Anonymity can be reduced through small or subdivided prisons (Wortley, 2002).

Considering the relationship between prison violence and the intake of drugs by inmates, substance abuse programs in correctional facilities will also be useful in reducing prison violence, especially the prisoner-prisoner assault. Available literature suggests that the type of treatment that is most promising are prison-based therapeutic communities that operate as segregated facilities within the facility (Dietz, et al. 2003).

Inmate Behavior Management

Correctional officers can take advantage of NIC training, technical assistance, and information resources on the design, and also the operation of direct supervision of jails and on key elements that are necessary for managing inmate behavior in all types of jails. These key elements of the training include assessing inmates' risks and needs (classification), assigning inmates to cells, meeting the basic needs of inmates, setting and conveying behavioral expectations, supervising inmates, and keeping inmates productively occupied.

The Napoleon Hill Project has also reduced violence in correctional facilities. It is a pilot program that was implemented by the North Carolina General Assembly in order to help the rehabilitation of inmates and aid in the reduction of recidivism by making use of a course of study based on developing positive mental attitudes. The project was utilized by the Blanch Youth Institution, Central Prison, Duplin Correctional Center, North Carolina Correctional Institution for Women, Pender Correctional Institution and Western Youth Institution. Inmates in the above-mentioned facilities can volunteer or be referred by staff for participation. Staff members that completed the Positive Mental Attitude Science of Success Program and have been certified by the Napoleon Hill Foundation serve as instructors for the eight-week course that seeks to ameliorate participants' self-esteem, self-assurance, and feelings of self-control.

Keywords: Violence, Correctional Facilities, Inmate, Prison, Prisoner, Guards, Assault, Crime, Sexual, Jail Administrators, Supervision, Surveillance, Misconduct, Violent, Staff, Officers, Contraband, Drugs, Victimization.

CHAPTER FOUR
Effective Methods to Prevent Escapes

The safety and security of correctional facilities provide benefits not only to the visitors to the correctional facilities, but also inmates, correctional officers, and the community.

> *"Secure prisons are essential to making our justice system an effective weapon against crime. When prisoners—convicted or awaiting trial—are entrusted to your care, they must know and the public must know that they will remain there until they are legally discharged... "*
>
> *(Nelson R. Mandela 1998)*

Correctional facilities have for some time focused on the control of inmates, basically through physical containment. This includes the use of steel doors, locks, alarm system and security glass, and it was believed that the safety of prison officers depends on the maintenance of physical barriers between inmates and prison staff; however, this approach failed to ensure the safety of correctional facilities and inmates. Vandalism, violence, and poor sanitation were problems that most inmates faced. The safety and control of inmates is possible when there is an established effective management of inmates' behavioral acts.

When the behaviors of inmates are effectively managed, then correctional facilities will equally be a good workplace for correctional officers, a great service to the community and also a clean and safe detention facility for inmates (Hutchinson, et al. 2009).

Methods of Prison Escape

One of the major factors that encourage the escape of inmates is the idle time they have to devise their escape. Correctional facilities have always corrected observed weaknesses after the escape of prisoners. There are common methods prisoners have devised to help them escape.

> *"You have to keep on target with everything, the inmates have nothing but time on their hands to think and observe the facility. If the same mistake is made consistently, it can eventually result in a disaster."*
>
> *(Ed Szostak, Superintendent of the Albany County Correctional Center)*

Deception

Inmates have escaped simply by deceiving correctional officers. Inmates could disguise themselves as prison staff or a civilian and escape from the prison without arousing suspicion. Some inmates also construct dummies in order to make correctional officers believe they are still in bed when they are not there.

Breakdown of Prison Facility

Inmates also escape by destroying cell or correctional facility compounds. They make use of items such as smuggled objects, homemade tools, and other items. They could slip through tight spaces, and on rare occasions, they dig a tunnel beneath the facility that leads outside the facility.

Exploiting the Weakness of Correctional Facilities

Inmates can escape from prison by carefully examining the weaknesses in the security system which in most cases are overlooked. This could include taking advantage of officers who ignore prison procedures and policies.

Assistance from Corrupt Officers

In some instances, inmates escape by taking advantage of corrupt officers. The assistance can be in the form of smuggling, and corrupt prison officers can smuggle in contraband and other items that could aid the escape of inmates. Inmates can also take advantage of the wrong actions of corrupt officers to plot their escape.

Escape With Help From Outside

Inmates can escape from prison when they are transported from one facility to another or when they are taken outside for medical appointments and hospitalization. They can also get help from an accomplice outside the facility; the help could be in the form of a ride or the provision of helicopters.

The Management Plan for Inmate Behavior

There are two major areas of the inmate behavior management plan. The first one, which was introduced by W. Raymond Nelson, is the Podular direct supervision. The second area is the inmate classification, which was also introduced by James Austin and Timothy Brennan. It consists of several elements outlined below:

- Assigning inmates properly to housing in the correctional facility.
- **Defining and conveying the expectations for each inmate's behavior** - There should be expectations set for inmate behavior in order to support the goals of the general inmate behavior management plan. Although expectations should be high, they should also be attainable, and such expectations should be effectively communicated to the inmates.
- **Proper supervision of inmates** - The inmates are held accountable for their behavior, correctional officers should interact with inmates to obtain a positive prisoner behavior and compliance with the rules of the facility.
- **Engaging inmates with productive activities** - The inmates need to be occupied with productive activities that place emphasis on the positive rather than the negative. They can be occupied in several ways, such as:
    - Permitting positive and unstructured activities within the housing unit, like the provision of books, magazines etc.
    - Assigning roles to inmates, like tidying their cell and cleaning the dayroom area.
    - Inmates should be encouraged to attend programs and utilize services outside the housing unit, like education classes and life skills programs.
    - Facilitate structured activities, like exercise, tournaments, and games outside the housing unit (Hutchinson, et al. 2009).

The establishment of these elements will serve as a continuous and integrated process that is designed to enhance positive inmate behavior which conforms to the expectations of correctional officers. It will also put correctional officers in control of the facility, rather than the inmates. The establishment of a formal and clearly written inmate behavior management plan will provide prison administrators with two things: an effective strategy for maintaining control over inmate behavior, and a mechanism for early identification of problem areas in inmate behavior (Hutchinson et al. 2009).

Assessment of the Needs and Risks of Inmates

This assessment needs to be done at various points while they are in detention. There is a need to obtain the information regarding the needs and risks of inmates; this is the first element in the behavior management of inmates. The risk is the extent to which the inmate is a risk to himself or herself and to others; it also includes the tendency of a likely attempt by the inmate to escape. The measurement of the psychological and physiological requirements for well-being (United Nations, 2015).

The method of assessing inmate risks and needs by a correctional facility is inmate classification. It is the responsibility of prison administrators to implement an effective inmate classification system which will properly assess the risks and needs of each inmate accurately to enable prison staff control and manage inmate behavior effectively. An effective inmate classification should possess certain attributes like equitability, validity, and reliability (Hutchinson, et al. 2009).

Risk Assessment Criteria

Basically, the escape risk implies the risk that an inmate poses to people when he/she escapes. In assessing escape risk, the following factors need to be considered:

- Warrants and detainees.
- The level of severity of the current charge of the inmate.
- Any additional charges and the criminal history of inmate.
- The status of the sentence; is it pre or post-sentencing?
- Does the inmate pose a potential threat to other inmates and correctional officers?
- The duration of the sentence, which usually indicates the nature of the crime committed.

- The possible threats that the inmate might cause to the community if he/she escapes.
- Any history of sentence abuse.
- Escape history of the inmate and the possibility of escape with or without external help.
- The family ties, age, residence, and employment of inmate.
- Institutional disciplinary history.

The needs of inmates are assessed in common ways and outlined below:

- Mental condition, which is psychological.
- The medical condition of the inmate.
- Any record of substance abuse.
- The intellectual capacity of the inmate.

(Hutchinson, et al. 2009)

Inmate Housing Plan

Another element in the inmate behavior management plan is the assigning of inmates to the appropriate housing, which helps prison staff to manage the inmates effectively. Prison staff utilizes the information about an inmate that was obtained during the assessment of risk and needs of the inmate. Several factors need to be considered when making a housing assigning decision (United Nations, 2015):

- The ability of an inmate to function with other inmates.
- The extent of the security risk the inmate presents.
- The need to consider the types of services the inmates require.
- What is the level of supervision the inmate needs?
- They also need to consider the legal requirements for separating certain classes of inmates, and these requirements vary from state to state.
- What type of programs should be made available to the inmate?

Meeting the Basic Needs of Inmates

The basic needs of inmates, which are just the same as other human beings, include:

- **Physical needs** - This includes the provision of basic needs, like protection against the elements, good food, medical care and others.
- **Safety needs** - The inmates should be protected from harm, which could be as a result of an unsafe environment or assault.
- **Social needs** - Inmates should not be isolated; they need to maintain contact with their friends and family.

Implementation of Inmate Behavior Plan

In order to effectively implement an inmate behavior management plan, there are several requirements needed:

- There is the need for staff training.
- There should be a systematic documentation of every activity that is related to inmate behavior management.
- There should be written and clear directives that will serve as procedures for each step.
- Adequate staffing is required at all levels.
- In order to ensure adherence to the plan, corrections officers should be supervised.

The implementation of the plan will require effective leadership of the correctional facility administrators, who will support inmate behavior management operationally and philosophically (United Nations, 2015).

Prison Intelligence

One of the fundamental parts of effective dynamic security is prison intelligence. A careful acquisition of information from prisoners, the observation, and monitoring of prisoners and the analysis of the information that was gathered should be the bedrock of preventing escapes and other criminal activities in correctional facilities. It is better to set in motion measures that will prevent escape from prison, drugs, and riots rather than deal with its aftermath (United Nations, 2015).

Physical Security of the Prison

There is a great need for the physical security of the correctional facility to be effectively planned. Setting a minimum physical security standard for each type of correctional facility and for each element within the facility is a good practice. There are several aspects of the physical security of a prison:

- It includes the walls and doors of the accommodation units.
- The bars on the windows are also very important.
- The strength of the building in the correctional facility.
- The watchtowers and specification of the perimeter fences and wall.
- Effective alarm systems.
- Metal detectors.
- X-ray machines.
- Locks and handcuffs.

There is a need for balance when designing the physical aspects of the prison security and the respect for human dignity (United Nations, 2015).

Procedural Security

Considering the physical fabric of some older prisons that has blocked lines of sight and poor visibility and the difficulty in the reinforcement of such structures to latest standards, it is important to complement these correctional facilities with other forms of security. In order to foster proper security and prevent inmate escape, effective procedures and systems of security are required locally and nationally. The application of procedures is very crucial in the prevention of escapes, and a fundamental aspect of correctional facility security.

A procedure is a process that has been standardized which serves as an approach expected to achieve consistency, fairness, regulation and help correctional facilities staff and managers to execute their duties (United Nations, 2015). They provide detailed information regarding special problems that could occur and usually include a checklist to render extra control that will ensure proper performance of the task. The human memory is prone to memory loss, and prison staff may forget how to execute a task that does not have a high frequency of repetition; this is why there is a need for procedures. Procedures should be clearly understood, and staff members should know how to execute certain security functions.

A procedure has the following features:

- Procedures outline how policies are executed.
- It involves a series of steps that are executed in order to achieve goals.
- In times of crises, they serve as a source of quick reference.

- They define the mechanism to help enforce policy.
- They form the basis for staff training and assist in eliminating the problem of a single point failure.
- Procedures are presented in a clearly written format that is accessible.
- Procedures are issued in good time to enable proper implementation.
- They are accessible, reproducible and available.
- Procedures should be short and not missing relevant materials.
- They can be updated and deleted.

The Security Framework of Correctional Facilities

Prison administrators should possess a state, national or federal high-level correctional facility security framework document which will provide correctional facilities with the much-needed information and guidance on how to maintain high levels of security and also prevent prison escapes. The prison security framework in many jurisdictions focuses on four major high-level security functions:

- **Assessment and categorization** - Despite the fact that inmates may not like their stay in prison, most of them accept the present reality; however, some inmates will do everything possible to escape. The risk assessment of inmates will ensure that inmates get proper security suitable for them.
- **Searching** - The major safeguard against smuggling is the initial searching of visitors on arrival, and when it is not done properly, this safeguard is lost. Searching procedures should be clearly written.
- **Accounting and control** - It is very important to have proper procedures and systems for accounting for inmates; it ensures the safety of inmates and staff members. A count refers to the physical acknowledgment of the number of inmates in a correctional facility. There should be a procedure that is established to know:
    - When to count inmates
    - Location where the count will be done
    - How the counting should be done
    - Who should count the inmates

- Plans for recording the counts
- Time for a prohibition of movement of inmates
- The counting procedures in case of emergencies

- **Communication and surveillance** - Communication in prisons must be effectively managed in order to inhibit trafficking of unauthorized items, prevent criminal activities, prevent escape of inmates and protect the public from unwanted communications (United Nations, 2015).

Prevention Strategies

According to Superintendent Ed Szostak, the following recommendations will help in the prevention of prison escape:

- **Proper Inventory Control** - There should be tight control over inventory of all types, such as tools and linens.
- **Ensure Adequate Supervisory Checks** - This includes not only supervisory checks, but also perimeter checks.
- **A Tight Access Policy** - This should be applied to staff and visitors; they should not be permitted to bring in anything that is not relevant to their job.
- **Shake Down** - There should be occasional total shut down of the facility to enable correctional officers to search the facility thoroughly.

General Movement Tips

Generally, the movement of inmates should also be monitored by putting a control procedure in place to ensure that inmate allocations are risk assessed, recorded clearly and controlled from a central point. The following points are worth noting:

- Designated movement routes should be agreed upon based on threats and risk assessments.
- The movement routes should be safe and also easily observed by CCTV, where available.
- Correctional officers supervising movements should be in radio communication.
- The movement pattern should be unpredictable and centrally controlled.

- The movement routes should avoid open areas or access to rooftops as far as possible.
- High-risk inmates should be searched on departure from each location and also logged out.
- The inmates should be logged in when they arrive at the approved destination.
- There should be no movement of individual high-risk inmates until mass movement of inmates is completed and a correct prison roll is obtained.
- A stand still roll check should be conducted if the roll is not correct. The roll check will take place at the particular location where there is a discrepancy.
- When this does not reconcile the role, then a stand still roll check should be carried out at every location.
- A situation where this does not reconcile the roll, all inmates should be returned to accommodation blocks for lock-down roll check.

If the prisoners' behavior is effectively managed, correctional facilities can be a great workplace for correctional officers and also a clean detention environment for inmates. The prevention of the escape of inmates also ensures the safety of the community, especially when the inmate is a high-risk prisoner that could be a threat to the peace and safety of the community. Procedures should be clearly set and followed to ensure that security of the facility is not compromised (Hutchinson, et al. 2009).

Summary

The major goals of jail security include the prevention of institutional violence, prevention of prisoner escapes and maintaining order within the correctional facility. In order to enhance security in the correctional facilities, there should be a combination of adequate facilities and security gadgets, appropriate staffing and well-defined operational procedures. The security of a correctional facility is determined by the class of inmates housed and the mission of the facility. The extent of the jail's security capabilities is based on several factors, such as the construction method and materials of the facility, the level of security equipment, perimeter security features, the staffing pattern and operations (Martin, et al. 2007).

An effective perimeter security will prevent inmates from escaping from the secure area of the facility and also serve as a barrier between the secure area of the facility and the outside world. It is also important to effectively monitor the security of the correctional institution, and this can be achieved through the use of several technological devices (Martin, et al. 2007). Some of the technological devices that will enhance the security of correctional institutions and also prevent the escape of inmates can be found below.

Effective updated technology is another key element to eliminating escapes and other numerous correctional deficiencies.

- **CCTV Off Site Monitoring:** The CCTV off site monitoring technology service can be invaluable. In order to effectively utilize it, there is a need to hire a CCTV monitoring company or correctional team staffed with current and/or retired alert correctional professionals that will help monitor jail and prison operations, movement, housing units, perimeters, tunnels and other areas of the facility that may be a security concern. In areas with limited access and movement, motion detectors should be used to alert the monitoring staff of movement. All possible escape routes, security areas, and known security areas should be assessed for possible use by motion detectors and CCTV technology. This unit can be on or off-site in a nearby secured location that has immediate access to communication with staff and/or management via email, text, phone or two-way radio in case of an emergency. This unit should provide a daily shift report that will express their concerns and praises to the appropriate managerial personnel.
- **Facial Recognition Software:** It is highly recommended that the high-tech facial recognition software is considered with the CCTV technology, especially at all entrance and exit points in order to detect inmates and other personnel that may be entering and exiting unlawfully.
- **Improved Human Detection Technology:** The MicroSearch® is a one-of-a-kind security inspection system that has the capability to detect human beings that may be hiding in vehicles or containers loaded on trucks, by sensing the vibrations of the human heartbeat (advertised on American Jail Association website 2016).
- **Proper Restraints:** All restraining mechanisms, including leg irons, handcuffs, and other devices, should always be checked for proper working conditions before use and double locked.

Wrongful Discharge Prevention Strategy

The discharge procedures at every step and level, including transport and records department, should have checks and balances and be reviewed often by management, audit team and outside correctional security consultant for possible security breaches. Mock escape exercises should be conducted with misplaced and/or erroneous paperwork to increase staff awareness and reduce the opportunity of an escapee who is wrongfully discharged by staff due to paperwork errors, undetected warrants, holds and inmates switching identification. This will be an opportunity to view the weakness and strength of the discharge process and make the proper adjustment as needed.

Managers of correctional institutions should seek for a comprehensive security audit of the facility if they have concerns about its effectiveness; the aim of the audit is to reveal any deficiencies in the systems, facilities, equipment or practices that may negatively compromise the security of the correctional institution. Adequate plans should be developed in order to resolve the identified deficiencies or lapses identified by the audit team (Martin, et al. 2007).

There should be good order and control in correctional facilities, which will be supported, directed and monitored by having management systems, policies, and processes in place. There is a need for an operational framework to ensure a consistent focus and the application of key security routines, adequate number of competent and trained staff and also standards that hold correction staff and prison management accountable.

Daily security routines, which include counting of inmates, searching, managing inmate movements, classifying and separating inmates, all contribute to good order in correctional facilities and also provide officers with the essential contact with inmates (United Nations, 2013).

Keywords: Efficacy, Technology, Control, Preventing, Inmate, Jail, Prison, Procedure, Escape, Correctional, Intelligence, Risks, Assessment, Security, Charges, Sentence, Correctional facility, Prisoner.

CHAPTER FIVE

Effective Methods to Control Gangs

The activities of prison gangs pose a serious threat to one of the major goals of the correctional agencies. The correctional facilities have a duty to ensure that inmates are rehabilitated, and if gang groups are allowed to freely operate, then that aim is no longer achievable. Gangs in prison disturb the programs of correctional facilities and also the safety of everyone in the correctional facilities, which includes inmates and correctional officers.

A prison gang is an organization that operates within a correctional facility as a self-perpetuating entity which is criminally oriented. A gang consists of a group of inmates and have an organizational hierarchy with a chain of command and established code of conduct. While they usually carry out their operations in secrecy, they also have a goal to execute their plans by maintaining control of the prison environment through violence. Intimidation which is usually directed at other inmates who are not members of the gang is also part of their strategies (Lyman, 1989).

> *"One thing we do know: prison gangs are gang researchers' final frontier and prison managers' biggest nightmare."*
>
> *(Fleisher, et al. 2001)*

The Level of Gang Involvement in Prison Violence

Despite the fact that it is not possible to have official data that will provide a good estimate of gang involvement in jail violence, it can, however, be argued that the involvement of gangs in correctional facilities will most likely be similar to gang involvement in the communities (Thornberry, et al., 2003; Maxson, et al., 2005).

Available data from the National Gang Investigators Associations reveals that the U.S. gang composition is estimated to be 85% street gang members, 9.5% correctional facilities gang members, and 2.5% outlaw motorcycle gang members. Although correctional facilities' gang activities are believed to be the least problematic, great care must be taken to control their activities to ensure that the goals of correctional facilities are achieved. According to the report, criminal proceeds from prison gangs are laundered through extortion schemes and tax fraud. Friends, family members and compromised prison staff are involved in prison gang activities and recruitment during a member's incarceration.

Examples of highly structured prison gangs include the Nuestra Familia and Aryan Brotherhood, while an example of a prison gang with less formalized structure is the Mexican Mafia (National Gang Intelligence Center).

Factors That Foster Violence in Prisons

Based on the results of several types of research made on violence in correctional facilities, several factors have been observed to be part of the causes of the increase in violence and gang activities in correctional facilities.

- **Management and Accountability in Correctional Facilities** - Effective management and leadership is vital to the survival of any organization. There is increasing evidence to suggest that poor control and prison management are the two main factors that influence both individual and collective prison violence (Ekland-Olson, 1986). Some of these poor management factors include: poor mechanism for grievance and dispute resolution, indiscipline among correctional officers, the unwillingness of officers to intervene in cases of violence and victimization, gang formation and several others.
- **The Size of Correctional Facility** - The size of the facility could lead to crowding, and there is evidence from studies conducted to suggest that violence thrives in confusion, density factors and crowded correctional facilities (Gaes, 1994; Ruback and Carr, 1993).
- **Inexperience of Staff** - It was discovered that work experience of

correctional officers and a disproportionate number of trainees getting assaults are among the four most crucial factors associated with prisoner-staff assault (Kratcoski, 1988).

- **Architectural Design and Violence** - Available results from several studies indicate that group cell prisons contribute to interpersonal violence, and especially when poor selection procedures exist (O'Donnell, et Al. 1996).

The Organizational Structure of Prison Gangs

Just like every other organization, prison gangs also have a well-defined organizational structure. A gang operating in the prison has an inmate designated as a leader of the gang; he supervises a council of members whose responsibility is to make the final decisions for the gang. The rank and file of the gang form a hierarchy, which makes the prison gangs more similar to organized crime, like their counterparts outside the prison (Decker, et al. 1998).

Gangs in correctional facilities have their unique symbols, motto and a constitution which prescribes the behavior of group members, and in order to be part of the gang, absolute loyalty and secrecy are required (Marquart, et al. 1997), (Fong et al. 1991). In order to promote a gang member, violent acts will be required. Drug trafficking is one of their major focuses, and if any gang member decides to leave, it is viewed by gang members as a threat to their security.

In a bid to prevent any gang member from leaving, prison gangs devised the "blood in, blood out" credo (Fong et al. 1992). An understanding of the structure of prison gangs will help correctional officers in developing effective strategies that will help them curb the violent activities of gangs in correctional facilities.

Dealing with Gangs and Violence in Correctional Facilities

As a result of the existence of gangs in correctional facilities, there will always be acts of violence. Every jail administrator needs to deal with such cases of violence with any of these effective strategies, depending on the one that fits the condition of the correctional agency.

Ensure There is Transparency

The aftermath of every inmate's experience in the prison has several effects, either positive or negative on the community and offenders. It is, therefore, necessary to develop a system of oversight which includes an external review of the activities in the correctional facility. The national performance measurement system was recommended by the Association of State Correctional Administrators, which is summarized this way: "what gets measured gets done" (Wright, 2005). Jail administrators will be compelled to develop effective measures to curb gang activities when they are aware that their performance will be evaluated based on the outcome measures (Gaes, et al. 2004).

Establishing Evidence-Based Practice

As a result of the low level of the application of best practices in dealing with gang violence in correctional facilities, there is a need for a national prison violence reduction initiative, which will consist of three steps:

- The first step is to conduct systematic evidence-based reviews of major prison problems
- Carry out a field test of several strategies that was designed based on the reviews
- By using rigorous evaluation designs, evaluate the strategies

Isolation of Gang Leaders

Isolation of gang leaders is one of the popular strategies used by jail administrators in dealing with gang violence and activities. When the gang leader is locked down, there will be a weak vertical communication within the gang, which will eventually lead to the loss of the gang's solidarity.

The Jacketing Strategy

The strategy of jacketing involves attaching a note in an inmate's file if the inmate is suspected of having any involvement with a gang. The inmate can be transferred to a high-security correctional facility. This strategy has been opposed by individuals who are of the view that a snitch could be responsible for giving out such information, and this could lead to the victimization of the wrong inmates.

Technology

Correctional facilities utilize databases that are used in tracking the activities of gang leaders and their members. Information about the gang includes: their digital photos, gang members' tattoos, scars and any other marks that can identify inmates that are obtained and recorded for investigation purposes. Considering the speed of accessing the database for relevant information about gang members, this strategy is very effective in curbing gang activities in correctional agencies (Gaston, 1996).

Restorative Justice-Driven Strategy

The results of recent research that was carried out on the application of this conflict resolution strategy to the problem of prison violence in England by (Edgar et al. 2003, 2005) provided promising results, even though they have not been rigorously evaluated. Social order in correctional facilities can be promoted by applying the following points:

- Fulfillment of inmates' basic human needs
- Putting in place several mechanisms to help resolve conflicts, such as restorative justice panels
- Striving to ensure personal safety
- Creating the opportunities to exercise personal autonomy

(Edgar, 2005)

The Measurement of Prison Moral Performance

Although it is necessary to monitor the performances of correctional facilities based on measures of violence and disorder, there is a need for the introduction of a new set of outcome measures which will recognize the need for a change of culture in correctional facilities. This change in culture involves the management staff, correctional officers, and inmates with the aim of improving the quality of life for everyone in the correctional facility. The outcome measures would have to focus specifically on the moral performance of prisons in several ways, such as:

- Daily prison routines
- Procedural justice
- Inmate-staff relations
- Access to treatment
- Distributive justice

Based on assumptions, it is expected that the improvement of the moral performance of correctional facilities will greatly affect the moral performance of prisoners when they are released to the community (Liebling, 2005).

Available results of a survey of correctional facilities by (Camp and Camp, 1985) indicated that when correctional officers were asked to choose the strategy that they may likely use against prison gangs, a total of 27 officers out of 33 correctional facilities surveyed cited the use of transfer, which relates to expelling gang members from the prison. Community efforts are crucial in curbing the menace of a prison gang, including strategies such as reintegration programs, which would offer specialized training and education for former inmates in order to help them meet the expectations of entry-level high-tech employment. Considering the fact that prison gangs' criminal activities also extend to the community, thereby allowing them to establish a stronghold in communities, such spread should be prevented (Fong and Buentello, 1991).

The control of gangs in correctional facilities does not only ensure the safety of the correctional agencies, but also ensures that the community is safe when the inmates are released. The efforts of correctional officers and administrators should be supported by community-based strategies aimed at ensuring the hitch-free reintegration of former inmates.

Summary

The results of a survey that was conducted by the Office of Juvenile Justice and Delinquency Prevention reveals that, in 2012, there were about 30,700 gangs in the United States, which was an increase when compared to 29,900 gangs in 2011. There was also an increase in the number of gang members, from 782,500 in 2011 to 850,000 in 2012 throughout 3,100 jurisdictions with gang problems.

The number of gang-related homicides increased by 20% from 1,824 that was recorded in 2011 to 2,363 in 2012. Other facts from the findings reveal that gang activities are concentrated primarily in urban areas in recent years, and there has been an increase in gang-related homicides nationally, partly as a result of increased reporting by correctional agencies (Egley, et al. 2014).

The identification of the reasons why inmates join gangs is a step in the right direction towards getting a solution to the issue of gang activities in correctional institutions. Some inmates join gangs in a bid to exert influence and also take advantage of other inmates, and this includes using any possible means, regardless of who gets hurt, to control their environment. There are inmates who also join gangs with the belief that they will be protected, which happens to be the opposite, because they get hurt by joining a gang.

One of the effective strategies in controlling prison gangs and their influence is the suppression of their activities, especially when the focus is placed on reduction of gang disorder, violence and the recruitment of new gang members within the correctional institution. Some of the suppression strategies include prison lockdowns, the separation and isolation of the gang leaders and the pre-emptive segregation of confirmed gang members (Trulson, et al. 2008).

It is important to carry out inmate assessment to determine if inmates are involved in gang or security threat groups, and such assessment can be done in several ways, such as the identification of tattoos, self-admission, written materials and other means. In controlling the gang activities, some questions need to be asked: does the inmate pose a threat to staff or other inmates? Is the inmate in need of protection from other inmates, or is the inmate a threat to the safety and security of the facility, staff, and other inmates? By compiling the results of the assessment, officers will identify the proper security level, program needs, housing of inmates and other needs which will help to ensure the safety of the facility, and also inmates (Campbell, 2014).

It is improper for inmates to be more familiar with the rules and regulations of the department than some corrections officers. Prison managers should ensure that officers are properly trained and also continue to receive training on how to deal with difficult and dangerous gangs in prisons. Correction officers also have to be updated regarding new information on how to deal with gangs (Campbell, 2014).

There is also a need for the establishment of the security threat group and renunciation and/or step down process, prison administrators need to also establish and implement the security threat group coordinator position. The coordinator will be responsible for collecting and monitoring security threat group records, information and also belong to the gang identification and validation and/or certification process. By providing a safe and effective renunciation and/or step down process, gang members or security threat group members will have the opportunity to return to the general population as long as they show commitment and demonstrate the willingness to discontinue from gang activity (Campbell, 2014).

Keywords: Prison Gangs, Violence, Gangs, Inmates, Criminals, Correctional Officers, Prison, Correctional Facilities, Approach, Strategies.

CHAPTER SIX
Effective Ways to Prepare for Prison Emergencies

Emergencies must arise, regardless of the efforts that have been made to maintain a safe and secure environment. An emergency could be any remarkable disruption of normal correctional facility order or routine, which could be caused by natural disasters, inmates' escape, fire or a riot. The occurrence of emergencies usually leads to serious bodily harm to people, including inmates and correction staff, and it can also lead to the destruction of the facility structures (Martin, et al. 2007).

Correction administrators and officers are responsible for the safety of the inmates that are locked up in the correctional facilities, and a quick and effective emergency response is very important, because the inmates have been locked up without the chance to save themselves from the dangers of the disaster. Ironically, most serious prison emergency situations are usually caused by the inmates that are locked up in the correctional facility. Every correctional facility has its first duty to protect the prison community, which implies that no matter the level of disaster or emergency, inmates must not be allowed to escape into the community.

The danger of a possible emergency is further worsened as a result of the problem of overcrowding in most correctional facilities, the decrease in the number of correction staff available and other factors. It is, therefore, important that considering the challenges faced during crises, jail administrators should acknowledge the dangers of major emergencies and commit serious resources, thought and time towards emergency preparedness (Schwartz, et al. 1996).

The Leader's Role in Emergencies

In crises and emergency situations, the leader has a very crucial role to play. The most important principle that will guide the jail administrator in the event of a major emergency is "drive your own agenda, or someone else will drive theirs." Despite the fact that the correctional facility could be in shambles and devastated, the leader must strongly develop a good and effective plan and pursue the plan aggressively (Schwartz, et al. 2005).

If the leader does not execute his plan, other forces, which are most likely external forces, will step into the situation, leaving the jail administrator and the correction staff in a reactive position, rather than being proactive. In driving his agenda, the jail administrator should take the following steps:

- The leader should thoughtfully develop a detailed step-down plan of action.
- Start a comprehensive inquiry into the factors that caused the crises and those involved in the crises.
- The leader should carry out a careful and thorough study of damage control and also establish repair priorities.
- The leader should have control over the media by establishing a firm control of the media relations and also create a proactive media plan.
- The leader should attend to corrections staff morale through staff briefings.
- The jail administrators should effectively communicate with the inmates and prevent any retaliation by corrections staff.
- The leader should candidly communicate with department officials and political decision makers frequently.

While making emergency plans, one of the factors to consider is the needs of corrections staff and their families; this also includes handling issues that have to do with traumatized inmates and their families. While it is very important that the leader should be well protected in a crisis situation, he needs to carry out his leadership functions in order to restore peace in the facility.

Reasons for Emergency Declaration

The declaration of a departmental emergency in a correctional facility can only be done by the director of the Department of Corrections; however, there are certain conditions that will lead to such declarations. Some of the conditions that could lead to the declaration of emergency include:

- When the lives of inmates, correction officers, and visitors are in immediate danger.
- It could be declared when there is a major natural disaster, like tornado, and acts of sabotage, such as a fire outbreak.
- It could also be declared in order to maintain a proper control of inmates or to handle the operations of key facility equipment, which seems to be beyond the ability of the correctional facility's resources.
- Emergency can be declared when there is a large-scale destruction of properties in the facility.
- When there are significant disturbances, which could be the massive escape of inmates or riots.
- An emergency can also be declared when there is a total loss of major utility service, such as water, communication, electricity, gas, etc.

Types of Prison Emergencies - There are several conditions in correctional facilities that could lead to emergency situations, and some of the conditions include:

- Power failure
- Hostage taking by inmates
- Riots
- Bad weather conditions
- Chemical spills
- Prisoner escape
- Bomb threat
- Fire

In setting tactical priorities during emergencies, correction officers and administrators need to consider the following people and tasks in their order of importance:

- The safety of personnel, the community or public, and the offenders.

- The incident should be contained and stabilized.
- Provide proper treatment for the injured while removing endangered people and those under threat.
- Reducing damages to a correctional facility and the expenses incurred (Law, Public Safety, Corrections and Security).

Emergency Response Plan

Every correctional facility should have a proper emergency response plan that will be useful in dealing with emergency situations; it is the foundation of emergency preparedness. The emergency plan should include several components, such as:

- **The Emergency Action Plan** - This is a roadmap that guides the actions of correction staff in their efforts to control and contain emergencies and also to provide adequate protection for prison staff, visitors, and the inmates. The quality of the plan determines the quality of the containment of emergencies.
- **Risk Assessment** - Correctional facility administrators do not have to wait for the emergency in order to prepare for it; they need to identify various types of emergencies that may occur in the correctional facility and develop appropriate measures that will help in controlling such occurrences.
- **The Organization and Coordination of the Emergency Response** - This process involves the provision of a clear process for making vital decisions during emergency situations and also the assigning of staff and the deployment of resources appropriately during emergencies. The execution of this component involves proper leadership qualities and discipline.
- **Adequate Resources and Equipment** - In order to provide an effective response to emergencies, the correctional facility should have sufficient equipment and resources, which include human resources. There should be adequate hands to help in dealing with the emergency situations and help prevent prisoner escape during the crises.
- **Drills and Training** - There is a need to train corrections staff on the effective use of devices and equipment needed during the emergency. The staff should also be trained on other aspects of emergency management, which includes the execution of emergency

plans. Staff members should undergo constant drills in preparation for any possible emergencies.

- **Recovery** - When the crises are over, the activities of the correctional facility need to return to their normal routine operations. There should be a well-defined strategy and plan for the full recovery of the correctional facility when the emergency is over.
- **Records and Reports** - The challenges and successes experienced during the emergency should be recorded to help in future planning and preparation. Considering what went wrong and how it can be effectively handled next time such an emergency occurs is a great way to deal with emergencies.
- **Review and appraisal** - After recording the events that took place during the emergency, the results of the report should be reviewed and evaluated in order to determine how well the correctional facility was able to handle the emergency.
- **Evacuation of Inmates** - In the event of life-threatening emergencies such as fire outbreak or other crises, an evacuation plan will be approved by an external inspector that is properly trained on the application of the national fire safety codes, which are reviewed yearly and updated when necessary. Inmates and staff should be evacuated from strategic exits within the facility in case of fire outbreak or other emergency situations (Martin, et al. 2007).

Benefits of Emergency Preparedness

Preparing for emergencies in correctional facilities will provide several benefits to the facility, which include:

- It greatly reduces the possibility of emergency situations.
- Emergency preparedness helps to mitigate the negative consequences that may arise as a result of the crises.
- It also helps to contain emergencies when they occur so as to prevent them from escalating further to major disasters that could lead to many casualties (Martin, et al. 2007).

Effective Ways to Prepare for Prison Emergencies

In order to effectively prepare for emergencies such as dangerous weather, fire outbreak, and others, the following actions will be useful in dealing with the emergency:

- Adequate food and water should be stored before a hurricane.
- Corrections staff should have an extra set of keys.
- Emergency lights should be installed strategically in order to provide light when there is a light outage.
- An effective communication system that is capable of projecting safe directions to corrections staff and inmates should be installed.
- In case of a tornado, an evacuation area should be provided.
- Extra staff should be requested to assist with the handling of prisoners to prevent any possible escape of offenders while the emergency situation lasts.
- Inmates that can assist other inmates to safety should be identified and involved.

Emergency Prevention

Considering the extent of damage and danger involved in prison emergencies, the best way to resolve emergency issues is the prevention of the emergency or stopping the crisis from escalating into an emergency. Although, every jail administrator and corrections officer totally agrees that prevention is the best approach, the efforts and commitment towards an effective prevention, when measured by resources, allocation and the management's degree of accountability, is amazingly low. Correctional facilities should be well prepared to respond not only to emergency situations, but also to any situation that could escalate into major crisis, and preventive activities should be part of the daily prison routine. Correctional facilities should also engage in strategies that reduce the possibility of a hostage situation, prison riot and any other crisis that may involve inmate violence.

> *"Good emergency preparedness can result in both prevention and mitigation."*
>
> *(Schwartz, et al. 2005)*

Although it may be difficult to state with complete assurance that all prison emergencies can be prevented, there are instances that are beyond human control, such as natural disasters, earthquakes, tsunami, and tornado. Despite the fact that it is not possible to completely prevent emergencies in prisons, the development of good emergency preparedness will greatly reduce the possible consequences of such emergencies (Schwartz, et al. 2005).

Strategies to Help Prevent Prison Emergencies

There are measures that have been designed to help prevent crises in correctional facilities, and some of them include:

- Training of corrections officers on how to identify the early signals of a possible emergency situation. The warning signs are usually part of the experienced staff members' "sense and feel" of the facility, which could be an unusual noise level in the facility, the intensity of staff-inmate interactions and several other warning signs.
- Being alert to "hot" issues that have the potential to cause dissension among prisoners. If hot issues are not properly handled, they have the potential to cause riots and crises within the facility. Obviously, a common problem that leads to crises in prisons is food; it could be issues related to a significant change in prisoners' food, giving them insufficient food or food that inmates do not like. These hot issues could easily lead to an emergency situation if not quickly resolved.
- The implementation of automated early warning systems can also help prevent emergencies. Automated early warning systems are computerized and designed to specifically "crunch numbers", analyze the data obtained and then send an alert to corrections staff when the information from the data analyzed indicate the possibility of crises.
- Avoiding agency-initiated emergency situations, such as actions that are initiated by the prison administration, could trigger crises in correctional facilities.
- Establishment of a prevention-specific intelligence function.

Traditional Warning Signs of Crises

Jail officers and administrators will find the following traditional warning signs useful in preventing prison emergencies:

- Increased request by inmates for protective custody.
- Increased hoarding of canteen goods or food by inmates.
- Increased number of racial groupings of prisoners.
- The refusal of inmates to go to the yard.

- A sharp decrease or increase in the rate of prisoner grievances.
- Increased cases of prisoners sending their personal items out of the correctional facility.
- High rate of sick calls by inmates and efforts to get to the infirmary.
- A remarkable change in the level of noise in the facility.
- A reduction in the inmate/staff interaction.
- Warnings of well-liked staff by inmates not to come to the institution.
- A reduction in the number of inmate visitors.
- Increase in the number of inmates wearing extra clothing in the yard (Law, Public Safety, Corrections and Security).

Features of an Effective Emergency Plan

An effective emergency plan should contain certain characteristics that make it very effective in handling major crises in correctional facilities:

- The plan should be practical and useful.
- It should be generic; it can be used effectively in other correctional facilities.
- A good plan should be consistent with established policies in the institutions.
- An effective emergency plan should be simple and easily understood.
- It should have a detailed step-by-step approach to dealing with emergencies.
- A good emergency plan can be tested if possible to ascertain its effectiveness.
- Emergency plans should be auditable to enable the management to ascertain its effectiveness.
- The plan should be open to inspection.
- A good emergency plan should be user-friendly, devoid of complications.
- It should contain checklists that will be easy for staff members to follow.

- Every part of the plan should be compatible with other parts of the plan (Law, Public Safety, Corrections and Security).

It is important that jail administrators and leaders develop a strategy for handling emergencies effectively; however, every emergency or crisis is unique, and therefore there may not be one plan that will be able to deal with all kinds of crises. What this implies is that, no matter how prepared a leader is for prison emergencies, it will not be a guarantee of a positive outcome. This, therefore, provides the leader with a realistic perspective that is required to effectively execute the plans for any emergencies. The most successful method of preventing crises in every organization which includes correctional facilities is to prevent the occurrence of such crises.

Summary

One of the major responsibilities of jail officials is the protection of inmates from harms caused by other inmates, staff, themselves or unsafe practices. The safety requirements of a jail are determined by its mission and also the custody category of the inmates that are accommodated in the facility. An effective jail security greatly depends on a good combination of the security capabilities of the jail and the custody level of the inmate population.

> *Good emergency preparedness can result in both prevention and mitigation*
>
> *(Schwartz, et al. 2005).*

The general trend in emergency preparedness is the use of a single generic plan which is also supplemented by appendices. There are several benefits of using a single generic plan; it is much easier to train correctional officers for a single plan than train them for six or eight different plans, and a single generic plan is less cumbersome and therefore more user-friendly than eight separate plans. Despite the level of improvements and strategies that correctional agencies have developed in prison emergency preparedness, there are serious challenges that jail administrators need to deal with in order to ensure the success of the strategies. One of the challenges facing emergency preparedness is emergency training, and this includes the initial and refresher training. Jail administrators need to ensure that new recruits are properly trained at the point of entry into the agency, and current officers should take refresher courses seriously to ensure their readiness for emergencies (Robbins, 2008).

A good emergency preparedness plan can definitely lead to the prevention and mitigation of emergencies, and it helps in the containment of emergency situations and violence before they escalate into major disasters. A good emergency preparedness should possess certain qualities: it has to be simple, it should not be too technical or sophisticated, it should be practical rather than theoretical and it has to be corrections-specific, which means it should be developed for correctional agencies. A good emergency preparedness should be user-friendly, tailored to each facility, auditable, detailed and field tested (Schwartz et al. 2005).

One of the major strategies to ensure that correctional agencies are ready for emergencies is the enforcement of strict adherence to emergency drills and exercises. It is invaluable to emergency preparedness, although many departments in correctional agencies have not been able to engage in a systematic program of drills and simulations due to the assumption that there are more pressing needs in the facility than the emergency drills.

The emergency drills should be part of the routine in prisons. Current global security issues have also made it compulsory to include a comprehensive consideration of an effective counter-terrorism response because of the densely populated nature of correctional agencies and also due to the fact that correctional facilities are symbols of government authority and several other factors. Jail administrators should ensure that there is a specific emergency preparedness procedure, especially for terrorist activities.

The current change in the tactics devised by terrorists around the world is a wake-up call to correctional officials to develop plans that are not conventional. Correctional officials will need to implement special procedures that may not be in a conventional emergency plan in the event of a chemical or biological attack (Robbins, 2008). Every department should also have an evacuation plan in case of fire or if the premises become uninhabitable.

Keywords: Emergency, Preparedness, Outbreak, Inmates, Corrections, Prison, Disasters, Prevention, Crises, evacuation, natural disaster.

CHAPTER SEVEN
Effective Classification Methods

An effective inmate classification process is very important to the successful running of correctional facilities and the safety of corrections staff and offenders. The classification process should be adequate to build confidence in the staff and also provide a clear working knowledge of what is really expected from inmates in order to move forward in the system. A major driving force of correctional facilities is an effective inmate classification process; it enables jails and prisons to meet one of their objectives, which is the safety of corrections staff and inmates.

Correctional facilities can meet this objective by rewarding good behavior with incentives while discouraging bad behavior with disincentives. When a classification plan is combined with programming, it will also help in reducing the rate of inmate recidivism, because inmates will definitely focus on the programming (Austin, 1998).

Inmate classification refers to the process of grouping inmates into different custody levels, which could be minimum, medium and maximum. The classification is done to match the inmate's needs with the available resources of the correctional facility. They are meant to differentiate inmates who may be a potential security risk or may have several management issues (Austin, 2003; Schmalleger and Smykla, 2001).

Types of Inmate Classification

There are two types of inmate classification, objective and subjective classifications. Subjective classification basically relies on the judgment and experience of jail administrators; they make the decision about where an inmate should be placed and the type of security and supervision an inmate gets while being incarcerated (Austin, 1998). Although this type of classification is not popular, it has not been abandoned because the use of "override" enables a jail administrator to alter the classification level of an inmate based on the policies of the agency.

The objective classification has several characteristics, such as:

- It is an inmate classification which ensures that the classification decision and the considerations are documented for examination and analysis.
- It is a valid and reliable criteria that have passed through empirical research and is useful in determining the inmate's custody level.
- Objective classification is carried out by specialized and well-trained correctional officers who make recommendations whether the custody level of an inmate should be maintained, increased or decreased and also provide a suggestion regarding the inmate's transfer (Austin, 1998).

Despite the fact that many factors which include length of sentence, drug, and alcohol use, the severity of the offense and other factors have little predictive capability for inmate risks, they are, however, given primary consideration in the inmate custody designation process (Andrew and Bonta, 2003; Austin, 2003). All inmates pass through the initial classification, internal classification and also reclassification process. The initial classification is regarded as external prison classification, which places inmates at a custody level where the inmate will remain while in jail. While some states designate custody levels, like minimum, medium and maximum, others use numbered levels, such as Level 1, 2, 3 and higher. Level one facilities are usually meant for inmates that possess the least level of danger to other inmates and to themselves (Gaines and Miller, 2003).

The Inmate's Individual Service Plan

As soon as inmates arrive, they are given a detailed and objective Individual Service Plan. The plan should define clearly the criteria for each inmate's forward and backward movement, and it provides a complete road map for the entire time an inmate is incarcerated. ISP provides the time frame that an inmate can make progress through the system and possibly the lowest security level an inmate can achieve too. The movement of inmates is based on their good institutional behavior, satisfactory performance and also participation in programming. Inmates are also enlightened about the negative impact disciplinary reports will have on their classification status and the severity of the setback when inmates get the disciplinary report.

14 Principles of Inmate Classification

There has been an increased emphasis on inmate classification as a management tool in correctional institutions. One of the widely accepted guidelines are the principles that were developed by NIC, and the 14 principles include:

- The goals and objectives of correctional system must be clearly defined.
- The classification process must be guided by detailed written procedures and policies.
- The classification process must make provision for the collection of high-quality, verified and standardized data.
- The testing and measurement instruments that are used in the inmate classification decision-making process must be objective, reliable and valid.
- There should be explicit policy statements that will structure and check the discretionary decision-making powers of the prison staff in the classification team.
- Provisions must be made to classify prisoners at the least restrictive custody level.
- Provision should be made for the screening of inmates and further evaluation of offenders who have management problems and also inmates who have special needs.
- Adequate provisions must be made to match offenders with programs, and the provisions must be consistent with the inmate custody classification.
- Provision must be made to involve inmates in the classification process.
- The classification procedures have to be consistent with the constitutional requisites.
- The administration and line staff should be given the chance to make input when there is a development of a classification system.
- The classification process must make provision for continuous evaluation and improvement.

- Provisions must be made for periodic and systematic reclassification hearings.
- A classification process must be economically sound and efficient (Austin, 1998).

The Inmate Classification Process

The inmate classification process varies based on several factors, such as the characteristics of the offender population and the philosophy and style of the jail administrators. Some of the inmate classification processes are explained below.

Intake and Booking of Inmates

Generally, the classification process of inmates in correctional facilities starts at the intake stage after an arrest has been made. Newly arrived inmates are placed in a holding area, which could be a cell or several cells, where they will stay for several hours or a few days. Offenders are searched and their personal items are taken from them, then they are fingerprinted and photographed. A record search is usually done to obtain relevant information about the offender, such as criminal history and warrants. Inmates also go through medical screening in order to ascertain if they need immediate medical attention (Austin, 1998).

Inmates' Initial Custody and Assessment

The initial classification of inmates is usually carried out after making the decision to detain the offender for arraignment based on the evidence to suggest that the offender will be detained for a substantial period of time. Inmates are usually separated into major groups due to diversity in the jail population. There could be male and female groups, juvenile and adult groups, sentenced inmates in one group and pre-trial inmates in another group.

Some jails also tend to separate the non-violent inmates from the violent inmates, inmates convicted of misdemeanors from those charged with felonies and also inmates with suicide tendency and other inmates with management issues are separated. Effective classification works with information obtained from interviews conducted, but reliance on self-reported data reduces the effectiveness of classification decision making, as the information may be inaccurate (Austin, 1998).

Inmates' Review for Reclassification

The reclassification of inmates is an important component of the entire classification process. While the initial classification makes use of items that describe the inmates' offense, demographics, and criminal history to determine the custody level of inmates, the reclassification criteria are basically dominated by the measures of the in-custody behavior of inmates. It is based on the premise that errors might have occurred at the initial classification stage, and such errors should be corrected based on the offender's current behavior. The reclassification of inmates is most likely a function of these four factors:

- The length of incarceration of inmate.
- The change in the status of inmate, from pre-trial to sentenced.
- Reclassification as a result of possible extra charges filed against the inmate. A reclassification can be done as a result of the satisfactory conduct of an inmate, and it could qualify the inmate for work release, a trusty position or other job placement, while unsatisfactory conduct could lead to a disciplinary hearing. A classification staff, inmates and shift commanders may request for reclassification.
- The conduct of the offender while in confinement.

Classification Designations

Inmates are assigned to different supervision levels based on several conditions and policies.

Maximum Custody

The maximum custody is reserved for offenders that have institutional behavior that will not enable them to function properly in general prison population, no matter the remaining time they will serve. Such behavior includes:

- Chronically disruptive inmates
- Violent offenders
- Predatory inmates
- Inmates that disrupt the safe operation of correctional facilities

Placing inmates in maximum custody has to be judiciously made as an exceptional case request which will be monitored by the facility classification committee at least every six months. The supervision of inmates who are placed in the maximum level custody requires that their movement in restricted areas will be under constant escort supervision with or without restraints, while their movement outside the security area will be with restraints, under the constant supervision of two uniformed officers (Inmate Classification System).

Close Custody

This type of custody is meant for offenders who have long minimum sentences, which could be 21 years or more. They also have serious escape risks and other inmate traits that require higher control in the general prison population. The custody of inmates in close custody is subject to review every five years of good observation in order to consider the reduction of the custody level. Usually, if a reduction is not granted after five years, then a review will be carried out yearly until the inmate is moved to a medium level custody. Close custody offenders cannot be assigned to programs outside the security area (Inmate Classification System).

Medium Custody

The medium custody level of inmates usually includes long-term moderate and low-risk offenders or marginal risk prisoners. At the medium custody, inmates are usually assigned to parole officers before a revocation hearing, and they also have escape problems. They have freedom of movement within the residency area, but with constant or intermittent supervision. Their movement outside the security area is also under escort and constant surveillance (Inmate Classification System).

Minimum Custody

This level of custody is for low-risk inmates with 48 months or less to their parole eligibility. They have through their institutional conduct demonstrated that they can conduct themselves with minimal supervision and control. They should have also been without any violent incidents within the last 12 months, and no attempt to escape from the correctional facility within the last seven years. There is a need for medical and mental examination and clearance before inmates are moved to a minimum-security prison, and offenders who refuse to be involved in available correctional programs in order to help identify and address their problem areas shall be excluded from the minimum custody. Inmates that have been identified as sex offenders and have passed through treatment needs to get clearance from the Administrator of the Sex Offender Treatment Program before they can be moved to minimum custody (Inmate Classification System).

Community Custody

Inmates who are kept in community custody are usually low-risk inmates who have satisfied the requirements for minimum custody and have 24 months to their discharge or parole eligibility. There is a need for medical and mental health clearance before inmates can participate in community service work lines. Offenders who refuse to be involved in the correctional programs available in order to deal with identified problem areas shall be excluded from community custody. Inmates at the community custody level have freedom of movement throughout with intermittent surveillance within residency areas, and their movement outside security areas within the perimeter is with or without escorts (Inmate Classification System).

Benefits of an Objective Classification System

The classification of inmates is a process of inmate placement in groups based on a rational plan or idea. It provides several benefits, such as:

- Reduced suicide attempts and actual suicides
- A reduction in the level of prison escapes
- Reduced inmate-on-inmate assault
- A reduction in the level of unnecessary confinement of non-threatening individuals
- Reduced inmate escape attempts
- Enhances a better and effective correctional facility operations
- Effective classification saves money by proper placement of inmates
- It enables the redistribution of corrections staff based on the custody needs of the inmates, and this gives room for better administration and management of crises.
- An objective classification system will ensure better security and control of offenders by providing effective surveillance and identification for each group and also assists jail officers in understanding the kind of inmate they are dealing with
- Effective classification provides the much-needed information for monitoring and evaluating program goals
- By identifying groups of inmates that may be eligible for several release programs, it helps in population management.
- Effective classification helps in the effective deployment of correc-

tions staff on the basis of an understanding of inmates' different custody and program needs.

- It provides inmate-specific data and standardized inmate custody profile information, which is useful in ongoing planning, management and policy development of correctional facilities

The proper classification of inmates is one of the important tools used in correction agencies to reduce or prevent the incidence of prison violence and other emergency situations that may arise as a result of high-risk inmates. Every jail administrator needs to ensure that corrections staff has proper knowledge of current classification trends. By assigning inmates to different custody levels, correctional facilities will be able to achieve their safety goals, both for correction staff and inmates (Austin, 1998).

Every correctional facility should have a detailed classification policy which provides clear criteria for forward movement of inmates within the facility and what type of criminal charges that will disqualify offenders for lower security custody, which includes minimum security or pre-release. Staff responsibility, appeal process for offenders and minimum requirements for certain statuses should also be defined in the policy. The periodic training of corrections staff to know about the criteria that are used in the classification policy is very useful in ensuring that inmates do not have more information than caseworkers and corrections officers.

Summary

Based on the information from the National Institute of Corrections (NIC), there are several guidelines that should be adhered to when correctional facilities are designing and implementing a classification system: there should be a clear definition of goals and objectives of the entire correctional system, and considering the fact that goals change over time, there should be a review of the classification system periodically in order to ensure that it is consistent with the current institutional priorities.

A manual of operations with detailed written policies and procedures that govern the classification process should be created. Correctional facilities should ensure that the classification makes provision for the collection of complete, verified, high quality and standardized data that will be used to monitor the classification process. The instruments used in the classification decision-making process should be measured and tested to ensure that they are reliable, valid and objective (Robbins).

There should be provision for systematic periodic reclassification hearings, which should be conducted at least once every ninety days in order to review new information regarding the changes in the prisoners' behavior, case, health, etc. A procedure that will be used for screening and further evaluation of inmates/residents that have special needs or who are management problems should be established. There is also a need for continuous evaluation and improvement of the classification process (Robbins).

A good inmate classification process should be efficient and economically sound. A good objective classification system should be simple in order not to interfere with other operational functions of the institution by overburdening the staff.

There is no classification system that is ideal for every tribe or correctional institution; however, a set of conceptual goals that are effective in designing a successful classification system, especially at the point of intake, includes:

- Every inmate/resident needs to be placed in the lowest custody level that is consistent with public safety.
- All inmates/residents should be classified based on objective information and also objective criteria.
- The classification process has to be uniformly applied so as to enable similarly situated inmates/residents to get similar custody assignments.
- The classification system must be able to provide centralized control over the process.

A successful classification plan should screen inmates based on several factors, like gender, age, the tendency for disruptive behavior, PREA concerns and finally, the governing charge that resulted in present incarceration. The correctional staff should be informed about what is involved in the screening and classification process, especially officers that have frequent contact with inmates. The Gang Intelligence Unit of the correctional facility needs to be used as a resource for inmate classification, because they will be in possession of the information on the dynamics between the groups in the facility that may cause dissension and/or disruption in the units. Information regarding the inmates' level of participation in their programming should also be passed on by the teacher or social worker to the board to assist in the decision-making process. An effective classification process ensures the safety of the professionals and inmates, and it should provide a clear working knowledge of what is expected of the inmates for them to move forward in their classification (Horgan, 2012).

Keywords: Classification, Reclassification, Assessment, Inmate, Corrections, Custody, Correction Officer, Offender, Objective Classification, Risk,

CHAPTER EIGHT
Effective Methods to Prevent Jail Rapes

Many people have the strong belief that inmates do not deserve any services and that prison rape is a kind of poetic justice or a form of punishment for the delinquent behavior of inmates. The public perception of rape in correctional facilities is that rape is an inevitable feature of confinement; however, rape is a crime that is violent and destructive, especially when the victim is incarcerated. Despite the efforts of courts and human right standards which are aimed at ensuring that people understand that inmates have the same fundamental rights to safety, justice and dignity like other people enjoying their liberty in communities, the victimization of vulnerable children, men and women sexually by inmates and correction officers still persists.

> *Sexual abuse is "not part of the penalty that criminal offenders pay for their offenses against society."*
>
> *U.S. Supreme Court*

The efforts to understand the scope and scale of the problem of sexual abuse of inmates is a recent development, even though the problem of sexual abuse is as old as the prisons.

> *A survey of State and Federal inmates suggests that about 60,500 individuals were abused sexually during the 12 months before the time of the survey*
>
> *(National Prison Rape Elimination Commission Report, 2009).*

With the passage of PREA, the U.S. Department of Justice is now able to collect data regarding the cases of sexual violence in American prisons. The results of a survey of the Federal and State prisoners that was conducted recently suggests that out of the 4.5% of inmates that were sexually assaulted during their incarceration, 2.1% were assaulted by other inmates, 2.9% from prison staff and 0.5% suffered a sexual assault from both (Beck and Harrison, 2007).

The Prison Rape Elimination Act (PREA)

The Passage of (PREA) in 2003 was necessitated by the problem of rape in correctional facilities, the underreporting and inappropriate response to the victims of rape and sexual abuse. It specifically addressed the problem of rape in correctional facilities and focused on supporting the reduction, elimination and also the prevention of cases of rape in correctional agencies at the local, state and federal levels.

The main goal of PREA is to support the reduction, elimination, and prevention of rape within correctional facilities at the federal, state, and local levels.

Targets of Prison Rape

Although all inmates stand the risk of violence and sexual abuse in the correctional environment, results from research conducted indicate that there are certain categories of inmates that are the potential targets of rape, which include:

- First-time offenders
- Young offenders
- Inmates who have small stature and those that are physically weak
- Lesbian, bisexual, gay, transsexual or intersex inmates
- Inexperienced and naive offenders who lack street sense
- Mentally ill inmates and also developmentally challenged offenders
- Inmates that have been victimized previously
- "Rats" and "snitches" and most prisoners that break the code of silence

Having an understanding of the possible class of inmates that are likely to be victimized is very important in efforts to prevent the incidence of prison rape.

(Hensley et al. 2005; Hensley et al. 2003; Dumond, 2000; Dumond, 2003)

Identifying Red Flags

Corrections officials are responsible for the effective supervision of inmates in order to learn about the behaviors of inmates under supervision. Considering the influence of the code of silence in preventing the report of prison rape cases and the stigma that is associated with rape, prison staff need to identify the "red flags" of sexual abuse which will serve as a guide to possible victims.

There are several effects of sexual assault on victims, and such effects which are termed "red flags" could be physical, psychological and behavioral. Emotional red flags of rape include:

- Depression
- Detachment and loss of caring
- Flashbacks and nightmares
- A loss of self-esteem
- Shame, guilt, and embarrassment
- Shock and denial
- Irritability
- A reduced interest in activities
- Impaired memory
- Suicidal thoughts

Some of the examples of the negative physical effects of sexual assault include:

- Vomiting
- Injuries
- Heart palpitations and sudden sweating
- Remarkable changes in sleeping pattern
- Nausea

Examples of possible negative behavioral effects of rape include:

- Self-mutilation
- Insomnia
- Eating disorders
- Increase in the use of violence and aggressive behavior
- Exaggerated responses to stimuli (adapted from National Center for Victims of Crime, "Sexual Assault")

There is a high level of a feeling of shame, loss of masculinity and humiliation by male inmates who have been sexually assaulted by other men (Robertson, 2003).

Sexual Violence in Correctional Facilities

Based on research findings, most victims of sexual assault in communities are reluctant to disclose the crimes to law enforcement agencies because of humiliation and shame associated with the incident, the fear of unbelief and the fear that other people, including family members, will know about the rape (Kilpatrick et al., 1992). Therefore, the estimation or measurement of the prevalence of sexual assault and rape in the community is a very difficult task. Experts are of the view that the high rate of discrepancies in the results of rapes and sexual assault in correctional facilities is associated with underreporting by the victims.

Apart from facing the same obstacles that victims of sexual assault experience in the communities, rape victims in correctional facilities also face other obstacles, such as the harsh realities of their incarceration, which includes the environment. A male inmate that has been sexually assaulted may find it difficult to disclose the incident, especially in an environment where physical strength means power, and also to avoid reprisal attacks. Rape victims in correctional facilities may not only fear that correctional facility officials do not believe them, but also fear that appropriate actions may not be taken even after they report the case.

Preventing Rape and Sexual Assault in Correctional Facilities

It is not possible for one individual to implement a change in a correctional facility. In order to establish cultural change, the efforts of everyone in the organization are required. One of the effective measures in preventing sexual abuse and rape in correctional facilities is the zero tolerance policy. (Zweig et al. 2007) Prison staff members can contribute greatly to zero tolerance and prevention of abuse within the correctional environment in several ways:

Have Professional Boundaries With Offenders Under Supervision

There are cases of staff sexual misconduct in correctional facilities, and one effective measure to prevent such issues from occurring is to establish professional boundaries with inmates when they meet, and it must remain that way throughout the duration of their supervision. There are other behaviors that corrections officers should avoid when they meet with inmates (Abner et al. 2009).

- They should avoid unnecessary meetings with inmates behind closed doors.
- Staff members should avoid extremely familiar behavior with inmates, which includes touching, though a handshake is allowed.
- Corrections officers should refrain from scheduling office visits that are outside normal business hours.
- Suggestive materials such as sexualized posters and calendars should be removed from the office environment.
- Corrections officers should avoid asking for personal favors from inmates, and they should also refrain from offering personal favors to inmates, such as overlooking the violation of the supervision requirements.
- As much as possible, officers should refrain from spending extended time with inmates in personal areas, like the restroom facilities and dorm rooms.
- Avoid the discussion of personal matters with inmates under supervision. Transporting of mixed-gender inmates should be avoided.
- Officers should avoid accepting gifts and giving gifts to inmates.
- Prison staff should not engage in sexualized conversation or inappropriate jokes with inmates.
- Report cases of inmates with red flags. Corrections staff members are expected to quickly report cases where the red flags are noticed to the proper authorities; this will help in dealing with the issue as early as possible before it escalates (Abner et al. 2009).

Sexual Abuse Prevention Rules

According to the final rule that was released by the Justice Department to detect, prevent and respond to sexual abuse in correctional facilities in accordance with (PREA), the following steps need to be taken to prevent sexual abuse:

- Prison facilities should develop and also maintain a zero-tolerance policy on sexual abuse.
- The corrections officials should screen offenders for the risk of either being sexually abusive or sexually abused.
- A PREA point official should be designated to coordinate compliance efforts.
- Train corrections officers on their duty in the prevention, recognition and response to sexual abuse.
- Document and develop a staffing plan which makes provision for proper level of staffing and video monitoring where applicable.
- Refrain from employing abusers and carry out background checks on prospective employees.
- Juveniles should not be housed with adult inmates, and they should not have unsupervised contact with adult offenders in common spaces.
- Incorporate unique vulnerabilities of gay, bisexual, transgender, intersex, lesbian and gender nonconforming inmates into screening and training protocols.
- Cross-gender pat-down searches of female offenders in correctional facilities should be banned.
- Inmates should be allowed to shower, change their clothing and also carry out other bodily functions without being watched improperly by corrections staff of the opposite sex.
- The use of solitary confinement as a means of protecting offenders that are vulnerable should be restricted (National PREA Resource Center).

Prevention and Technology

Prevention of Rape and Sexual Abuse can be enhanced with the use of technology. In Kansas for instance, video surveillance was used to prevent sexual misconduct. There are also several installations of monitoring equipment that will aid in the fight against rape and sexual abuse. Correction officers reported that inmates feel more secure with the increase in the number of cameras installed within the prison facility. In some instances, the use of Visual Tracking Grid has also proven to be a very effective tool in tracking gang activities, violent activities, sexual assaults and any form of suspicious activity in the correctional facility. A major advantage of the tracking grid is its ability to document "blind spots" that are located within the correctional facility. Blind spots refer to areas that corrections officers cannot see easily.

Several states in the United States have developed automated systems that enable them to track any incident of rape and sexual abuse by time and location, like the Connecticut's Statistical Tracking Analysis Report and the Pennsylvania's Web-enabled Timeline Analysis System. These devices and systems are not only used by states to document any incidents, but also useful in the development of strategies that will help in preventing the future occurrence of sexual assault and rape. The use of technology in the prevention of rape by correctional facilities should be encouraged by government at all levels. A combination of different strategies is a more effective strategy for the prevention of rape in correctional facilities (Zweig et al. 2007).

Although it is important to identify and also address potential concerns and limitation, it is also important to acknowledge and build upon the resources and strengths in meeting the needs of prison rape victims. There should be a collaboration with community allies, correction officers, and others. It is integral to the prevention of prison rape and in reaching victims. A combination of several strategies will be a very effective way of dealing with prison rape and sexual assault.

Summary

In 2011, a total of 8,763 allegations of sexual victimization was reported by administrators of correctional facilities, which was a significantly higher number than the 8,404 allegations recorded in 2010 and 7,855 in 2009. This increase has been constantly rising since 2005 mainly as a result of the increase in prisons, and it was also reported that 18 percent of the victims of inmate-on-inmate sexual victimization sustained injuries, while there was a reported case of less than 1% of incidents of staff sexual victimization (PREA Data Collection Activities).

Based on the information gathered from research findings that conducted a series of interviews and roundtable discussion with administrators and staff, it was discovered that there are 11 practices that have very promising positive effects in the prevention of prison rape. The eleven practices that correctional institutions need to adopt or strengthen include:

- A good leadership should promote values that foster dignity, safety, and respect for staff, inmates, and all residents. Effective leadership is essential to establish and enforce values that will reduce the incidence of prison rape, and good leaders have competent officers around them and also ensure that they constantly get trained on the job.
- The establishment of open communication between the managers and correctional officers and also between correctional officers and inmates and residents. Considering the fact that people are more comfortable talking to people like themselves, it is important that during the recruitment process, officers who come from a variety of backgrounds, religions and ethnicity should be considered in order to foster effective communication.
- The need for corrections officers to actively seek better ways that the prison population can be managed and also integrate ideas and knowledge from different sources, which include staff, accreditation process, professional associations and other facilities and agencies. New information is constantly being introduced into the field of corrections, and leaders should be ready to accept new information in order to increase the ability of the corrections officers to provide a safer prison environment and better services to inmates.
- There is the need for standardized and ongoing corrections staff training in order to transmit values through policies and practices.
- The recruitment and hiring of people with effective communication skills, mentoring and succession planning and also having respect for other people. *"Correctional agencies must engage in a staff selection process that is standardized and job-related, actually evaluating an individual's abilities and potential performance"* (Honnold, 1985).
- A good classification system that will ensure the safety of the correction staff and inmates.
- There should be a comprehensive and independent process which emphasizes key areas like training the security, medical staff and investigation on how to respond properly to rape victims, training them on the effective investigation techniques and promoting cross-training. The need to respond immediately to all reports of sexual

assault and all incidents of sexual assault should be investigated. Responding to victim sensitively and when appropriate, criminal behavior should be prosecuted.

- A direct supervision architecture and direct supervision principles for the behavior management of inmates and residents.
- Establishment of programs and services that will productively occupy the time of inmates, improve the life outcome of offenders and meet the needs of juveniles and inmates.
- The need for officers that are committed to detecting and correcting their mistakes, learning from litigation and are committed to transparency.
- The need for an effective system of data collection, analysis and an incident tracking system that enhances effective, data-driven decision-making.

Facilities where officials aimed to provide an environment safe from small aggressions and abuses were inherently safe from more intrusive assaults, including sexual assaults. For this reason, this study found that fundamental approaches to personal safety, for residents, inmates, and staff, were key elements critical to the successful implementation of PREA (English et al. 2011).

To prevent jail rapes, it is important to have staff as PREA trained auditors and PREA coordinators. There should be improved classification that will ensure that potential predators and potential victims are not housed together; such classification should be dynamic and objective and should recognize that the safety needs of individuals are unique when compared to the general traits that could place someone at risk. The classification should include a screening of inmates for the risk of abusiveness and victimization, which also includes the consideration of the traits that are known to place people at risk and also the individual's perception of vulnerability (Rothstein, 2009).

Keywords: Sexual Abuse, Rape, Officials, Correctional Facilities, Offenders, Inmates, Prevention, Assessment, Screening, vulnerable, Prison, Jail, Victims, Victimization

CHAPTER NINE
Effective Ways to Manage Mentally Ill Inmates

There has been a recent increase in the number of mentally ill inmates in a substantial portion of the prison population. This has led to serious therapeutic and administrative challenges to prison administrators and also mental health professionals. There is evidence to suggest that this is not just an increase in the population of mentally ill inmates, but also an increase in the seriousness of their illness (Adams et al. 2008).

> *The problem of mentally ill inmates in prison is serious and substantial, and indications are that the situation may be getting worse.*

Although the population of the United States is five percent of the world's population, the U.S., with 2.2 million inmates confined in various prisons, makes up 25% of the world's prison population. There has been a steady rise in the number of people with psychiatric disorders since the 1960s due to the deinstitutionalization of the state mental health system, which released about 90% of psychiatric patients into the community with inadequate support services (American Psychiatric Association, 2004; Fellner, 2006; Treatment Advocacy Center, 2007). Many of the patients became involved with the criminal justice system, which has made the three largest psychiatric institutions in the U.S to be:

- New York City Rikers Island, with 13,500 patients

- Los Angeles County Jail has 17,000 patients
- Cook County Jail in Chicago has 9,000 patients

The correctional facilities in the U.S. are now mental health institutions (Parker, 2006).

Reasons for High Number of Mentally Ill Inmates

There are several factors that have contributed to the increase in the number of mentally ill inmates:

- One of the reasons is the absence of adequate community support programs for individuals having mental disorders.
- There is also a serious issue of underfunding of public services.
- The downsizing or closing of state psychiatric hospitals.
- The lifestyle and poverty level of affected people, which makes them encounter the police.
- There is a tendency that mentally ill persons are adults with co-occurring substance abuse disorders.
- The presence of restrictive insurance and managed care policies which reduce the access to intensive services (Sundram, 1999).

Challenges of Mentally Ill Inmates

There are several issues correctional facilities face when handling mentally ill inmates, and one of them is the issue of staff limitation. Inmates with mental illness require more jail staff supervision than other inmates. They also need specialized medication, care, and monitoring. There is, therefore, the need for proper training of correctional officers to enable them to handle mentally ill inmates effectively.

- There are several challenges that prison administrators also face when handling mentally ill inmates. One of the challenges is the delicate act of balance that administrators have to consider when dealing with mentally ill inmates. This is because correctional officers are not supposed to punish mentally ill inmates for behavior that is beyond their control. There are also some mentally ill inmates that may not be able to clearly understand the rules or even perceive that the rules have been violated (Faiver, 1998).
- Even the healthiest of suspects finds going to jail difficult, and inmates who are mentally ill will find it more stressful when they

end up behind bars. The rapid change in environment and other external factors cause the patient to lose focus on their treatment plan and rather focus on their criminal charges.

- Another major challenge of handling mentally ill inmates is the high cost of maintaining them. The cost of taking care of mentally ill inmates is more than the cost of handling non-mentally ill inmates due to several factors, such as psychiatric medication, examinations and the lawsuits that have been on the increase.
- The tendency to commit suicide by mentally ill inmates is higher than non-mentally ill inmates. Evidence from a 2002 study in Washington State suggests that there was a 77% rate of attempted suicide among mentally ill inmates compared to a 15% rate among inmates.

Handling mentally ill inmates requires extra care, and the safety of correctional officers when dealing with them is always a major challenge, because they are more volatile than inmates without mental illness. Officers should be properly trained to handle such volatile situations without getting hurt in the process.

Identification and Screening of Mentally Ill Inmates

The first major challenge that correctional facility administrators face is the identification of mentally ill inmates. When they are identified early, it provides a better opportunity to save officers and other inmates from violence. Identifying mentally ill inmates will require the process of screening the inmates and assessing them before they are finally admitted. There are several points where inmates are screened in order to identify mentally ill inmates; however, the most widely used point is the intake. The Bureau of Justice Statistics reported that in 2000, about 70% of state prisons actually screened inmates at the point of intake for psychiatric illnesses (Beck & Maruschak, 2001).

Several practices and instruments have been developed over time to reduce human judgment, such as clinical evaluations and interviews and actuarial approaches. There are several reasons for the evaluation of inmates at intake:

- To enable correctional officers to identify inmates with mental health issues early.
- It provides them the chance to also spot potential mental health problems.

- By evaluating their mental health, they will be able to evaluate them for possible treatment.
- Identifying mentally ill inmates early will help reduce the danger they pose to themselves and other inmates.

There have been remarkable developments regarding the screening and assessment of inmates. This includes the debate over the level of accuracy of the use of actuarial versus clinical prediction models. The stakeholders placed emphasis on the ability of the models to predict the dangerousness or criminal recidivism of mentally ill inmates. Although, they agreed that statistically based actuarial model is believed to be more efficient in predicting a likely violent inmate or inmates that might likely reoffend, (Monahan, 1996) argued that the model should replace clinical approaches rather than being used as a supplement.

Based on the NCCHC standards, there are two levels of mental health screening in prisons. The first screening should be done within two hours of inmates' arrival. It should be executed by qualified health care personnel, certified by the state to support the duties of physicians. The second level of screening which is a post-admission mental evaluation, is recommended to take place within 14 days of inmates' admission, and it should be carried out by qualified mental health personnel, which include: psychologists, psychiatrists, nurses, physicians and others permitted by law.

Elements of Mental Health Evaluation of Inmates

An evaluation of the mental health of inmates should involve an interview that will inquire about the inmate's history and present condition with respect to symptoms and several factors. Such elements should include:

- Suicidal history
- Any history of sex offenses
- The inmate's current suicidal ideation
- History and current drug and alcohol usage
- The inmate's psychiatric history, and this includes hospitalization and outpatient treatment
- There should be a test of intelligence for mental retardation
- Any history of cerebral trauma or seizures
- Any previous case of victimization by criminal violence
- Any current use of psychotropic medication

- History of a special education placement (required by NCCHC guidelines 1999)

The Role of Correctional Officers

Correctional officers play a very important role in the effective management of mentally ill inmates. Several discussions have been made regarding their role, especially with respect to conflicting goals between custody and treatment and its effects on correctional officers. (Dvoskin and Spiers, 2004) developed a four-part multidisciplinary approach which is more elaborate to delineate the activities of correctional officers when dealing with the mental health treatment of inmates. They explained that correctional officers can be involved in the health treatment of inmates in several ways outlined below:

- Medication
- Consultation - This relates to talking about inmates
- Counseling and Psychotherapy - This has to do with talking with inmates
- Special activities, housing, and behavioral programs

According to Dvoskin and Spiers, correctional staff should be ready to execute any of the activities outlined above, which will provide two benefits; it will reduce the stress on inmates and staff and also greatly improve the quality of the mental health services that are rendered.

The Participatory Role of Correctional Officers

The participatory role of correctional officers in the mental health treatment of inmates has been viewed as an emerging paradigm that has great prospects (Appelbaum et al. 2001). The reason for this view is that correctional line officers have the opportunity to interact with inmates and through that process observe their behaviors throughout the day. This provides the opportunity for officers to be able to identify conduct or behaviors that suggest mental illness.

Rather than using the current trend where officers view inmates as a security threat, officers should imbibe the multidisciplinary treatment approach that will identify the mental health problems of inmates on time. This approach can be practiced through training and development of a shared value system between mental health staff and security staff, which is based on a common goal. Correctional officers should become full partners in the multidisciplinary approach to treatment. They should be involved in improving the operations of the institution.

Treatment and Control of Inmates

One of the critical management issues in handling mentally ill inmates is the relationship that exists between control and treatment and maintaining an appropriate balance between the two objectives.

> *"There is no 'one-stop shopping' offender typology available that can identify the risk level, targeted treatment protocols and control levels."*
>
> *(Byrne and Roberts, 2007)*

Considering the absence of such typologies, prison administrators and clinicians making evaluations and professional judgments that aim to balance concerns of treatment risks and effectiveness will play a vital role in the development of effective treatment strategies for inmates that are mentally ill. While making evaluations of inmates, prison administrators are likely to focus on the information that concerns the safe management of the correctional facility, while clinicians will likely focus on diagnostic-related information.

Effective Treatment and Risk Management

Mentally ill inmates have been identified as a special group of offenders that need a different approach in order to effectively handle their problems (Byrne and Roberts, 2007). Byrne and Roberts are of the opinion that rather than thinking in terms of mutually exclusive strategies which could be to change or control the offender, we can reduce the possibility of mentally ill inmates reoffending when the right treatment is provided. The implication of this perspective is that treatment is viewed as a kind of risk management that enhances public safety. The combination of risk management and treatment has to be introduced at intake to the correctional facility and also last throughout the treatment program.

Therapeutic Environments

The environments of prison facilities vary; while some of them are quiet and reserved, others are active and noisy. There are also some correctional facilities that are safe and predictable, and the conditions of the environment varies from cell block to cell block. Inmates should be able to discover specialized environments where they function better. It is possible to utilize this specialized environment and reduce stress in inmates from a therapeutic perspective (Toch, 1992). There are specific environmental triggers for irritable aggression, and aggressions of this nature are usually in response to an insult or frustration (Ax et al. 2007).

The Use of Medication

It is a common practice to treat mentally ill inmates with psychotropic drugs. In 2000, the U.S. Bureau of Justice Statistics reported that 73% of state prisons distributed psychotropic drugs to mentally ill inmates in their facilities. It was estimated that about 114,400 inmates received psychotropic drugs while in prison (Beck & Maruschak, 2001). Drugs are usually the first choice of treatment modality in prisons.

> *"Mental health interventions in the correctional setting are generally limited to psychiatric medications due to limits on space, time and/or money."*
>
> *(Parker, 2006)*

Effective management of mentally ill inmates is important to the successful rehabilitation of inmates and also a safer society. Mentally ill inmates have the highest rate of reoffenders, and this has negative effects on the society. Correctional officers need to be properly trained for maintaining the mental health of inmates, but presently, there is an infrequent rate of training of officers. Based on information from research, few numbers of training for correctional officers have the potential to produce remarkable rewards with regards to correctional facility management. The paradigm of correctional officers as predominantly security-focused personnel needs to be changed to a correctional approach, and they need to embrace mental health treatment responsibilities (Adams et al. 2008).

Summary

There is a significant level of involvement of people with mental health needs in the U.S. criminal justice system. This has led to the world's highest rate of incarceration and has greatly strained the social and economic fabric of several communities and also reinforced racial and class inequalities. It is estimated that about 400,000 inmates incarcerated in the United States suffer from some type of mental illness. This population is larger than the cities of New Orleans, Cleveland or St. Louis, and based on the information from The National Alliance on Mental Illness, it is estimated that between 25 and 49% of all mentally ill Americans will be incarcerated or jailed at some point in their lives (Ford, 2015).

Mentally ill offenders have special needs; however, most times they cycle through the criminal justice system without proper care that will address their mental health (Kim et al. 2015). About 56 percent of state prisoners, 64 percent of jail inmates and 45 percent of federal prisoners have mental health problems, and most of these individuals often receive inadequate care, with just one in three state prisoners and also one in six jail inmates getting mental health treatment since they were admitted (James and Glaze, 2006).

Majority of these mentally ill inmates had been arrested for crimes of survival, which includes retail theft that will provide them with food supplies or breaking and entry in order to find a place to sleep. There have been several interventions aimed at reducing the escalating levels of contact that mentally ill individuals have with the U.S. criminal justice system, and some of the interventions include criminal justice models like crises intervention and mental health courts, and there are mental health programs like the Forensic Assertive Community Treatment (FACT) and specialty probation models.

Despite the number of interventions, the high rate of mentally ill inmates still persists. There is an increasing number of scholarly literature which is of the view that prevailing interventions have been unable to achieve their goals due to the fact that they operate on a faulty premise:

> *"that people with serious mental illness engage in criminal behavior primarily because of their mental illness."*

Researchers from several fields have developed different alternative models in response to the doubts about the level of effectiveness of the present interventions. The new models are sensitive to social context and to several factors that tend to overlap with mental illness. These models focus on the circumstances in which people are born, where they grow up, live, work and their age.

There have been remarkable improvements in reducing the disruptive and negative life consequences for individuals experiencing the first episode psychosis. This approach is the prevention and early intervention approach. The reason for the early detection and intervention in mental health is quite obvious. Psychotic disorder is capable of derailing a young person's academic, social, and vocational development, which leads to cumulative disability and social marginalization.

It is therefore important, that the interventions for mentally ill individuals with an early criminal justice involvement need to take place before their incarceration in order to deal with their special needs. This approach of prevention is believed to be better than the system of late-stage intervention, rather than use a system that provides high-quality interventions to individuals when they have become difficult to serve. A front-end early intervention should be used.

> *"Front-end, comprehensive, recovery-driven interventions have real potential to disrupt a path of criminal justice involvement. Such interventions envision people as citizens, and not only as justice-involved."*

The use of recovery-informed practice is effective in the recovery process of people with mental illness, especially those at the early stage of involvement in the criminal justice system. The practice should include four elements, it must be trauma-informed and trauma-specific, because trauma has a significant role in the development of health issues. This involves the creation of trauma-informed locations where individuals can access services. The second element is for practitioners to endeavor to make mental health and criminal justice labels secondary to the treatment of their clients. The third element is that the recovery-informed approach needs to go hand-in-hand with a wellness approach, which places focus majorly on people and understands the impact of social determinants on the quality of their life and also empowers them to focus on self-care. The final element is the room for significant improvement in integrating peers and family into this work, because family members are always eager to assist their loved ones but may be prevented by the system.

The front-end, comprehensive and recovery-driven interventions possess the resources to disrupt the path of criminal justice involvement by focusing on valued activities like schooling, employment, and social connectedness that most individuals pursue. This kind of intervention sees people as citizens, and not just as justice-involved (Pope et al. 2016).

Keywords: Correctional Facility, Prison, Management, Mentally ill inmates, Treatment, Evaluations, Reoffending, Training, Mental health, Screening, Assessment.

CHAPTER TEN
The Effects of Long-Term Isolation and Therapy

There are several terms that have been used to describe the isolation of inmates, and these include solitary confinement, separation, and segregation. The isolation of inmates is a kind of confinement where inmates are kept in a cell alone and may be permitted to go out for an hour, though not in all cases. The isolation of inmates is usually meant to serve as a safeguard solution for prisoners who are problematic, but when it is used as a tool for punishment and deterrent, it is regarded as penal isolation (Cohen, 2008). Correctional facilities in the United States presently use penal isolation in Supermax prisons as an essential tool for controlling offenders that are troublesome (Smith, 2008).

Penal isolation usually leads to unanticipated and dangerous consequences to offenders. When such confinement is not carefully monitored, inmates will psychologically decompensate, thereby making them more dangerous to other inmates and themselves due to the extended isolation (Kupers, 2008). Supermax jail facilities make use of violent behavioral management strategies, and this could be the use of rubber bullets, cell extractions, tear gassing and electric Tasers (Toch, 2008).

When prisoners become a threat to the safety of other prisoners, the use of isolation will be the most appropriate solution in order to separate them from the main prison population; however, inmates that have been moved to Supermax prisons may remain there for many years without the re-examination of the inmate to determine if they still need to be isolated (Lovell,

2008), and this will lead to serious mental illness (Grassian, 1983; Haney, 2003; International Psychological Trauma Symposium, 2007).

Negative Health Effects of Isolation

There are several negative effects of isolation of inmates; apart from having a negative effect on inmates, it is also a threat to the community (Kupers, 2008). Most inmates that have been released after several years of incarceration may experience irreparable psychological effects of the solitary confinement, like the inability to make eye contact, psychosis, acute anxiety and a fractured self-concept (Haney, 2009). Other negative effects of inmate isolation include:

Physiological Effects of Isolation

Most inmates in solitary confinement are denied access to sunlight, fresh air and they experience a longer period of inactivity, which likely causes them to experience physical consequences. Some of the signs and symptoms that have been recorded as effects of inmate isolation include:

- Back and joint pains
- Insomnia
- Heart palpitations
- Lethargy and weakness
- Deteriorating eyesight
- Sudden excessive sweating
- Tremulousness
- Weight loss, poor appetite and in some cases, diarrhea
- The aggravation of pre-existing medical issues

Psychological Effects of Inmate Isolation

The most commonly reported effects of inmate isolation are the psychological effects, and it usually varies based on the pre-morbid adjustment of the inmate, the length of confinement, context, and conditions of confinement. Chronic symptoms may occur after the initial acute reactions of the inmate if the solitary confinement persists. Although some inmates may be more resilient to the negative effects caused by their isolation, others experience the negative effects outlined below:

Anxiety problems may include:

- Anxiousness
- Panic attacks
- Fear of impending death
- Persistent low level of stress

Depression problems such as:

- Hopelessness
- Mood swings
- Emotional flatness
- Major depression
- Social withdrawal

Anger problems may also include:

- Poor impulse control
- Unprovoked anger
- Outbursts of physical violence against themselves or others

Cognitive issues may include:

- Poor memory
- Short attention span
- Disorientation
- Poor concentration

Why is Inmate Isolation Harmful?

There are three main factors that are inherent in inmate isolation: loss of control over virtually every aspect of the inmate's daily life, social Isolation, and environmental stimulation. These three factors make up a potent mix (Shalev, 2008).

Social Isolation

The World Health Organization sees social well-being as integral to the definition of health; however, inmate isolation makes it impossible for an individual to stay in the midst of other people, and this deprives them of any meaningful physical contact and sympathetic social interaction. Most times, isolated inmates have been deprived the chance to communicate with other inmates and with a restriction on their interaction with members of their family and friends.

Social learning theories emphasize the value of social contact with other people, not only for the sake of play and pleasure, but also for the individual's sense of self that is shaped through social interactions. Social isolation of inmates may lead to further withdrawal. This position is supported by a study:

> *"seclusive" personality, "generally considered to be the basis of schizophrenia, may be the result of an extended period of 'cultural isolation', that is, separation from intimate and sympathetic social contact."*
>
> *(Faris, 1934)*

> *"seclusiveness is frequently the last stage of a process that began with exclusion or isolation which was not the choice of the patient."*
>
> *(Buss, et al. 1969)*

When an inmate is deprived of any reasonable interaction and sympathetic social contact with other inmates, the isolated inmate may withdraw and regress, and most times, they become uncomfortable with social situations when they are finally released.

Reduced Stimulation and Activity

Part of the experience of solitary confinement is reduced stimulation and monotony. Isolation in the 19th century allowed inmates to work, but in modern sections of solitary confinement, inmates may be restricted or deprived of any form of diversions, such as the television, radio, books or work.

> *The utter and monstrous boredom that becomes so obvious after a short period of isolation is an all-powering one...in order to fight off the tendency to complete idleness and to retain a hold on the senses, it is necessary to make great exertions...yet no matter how successful a prisoner may be in staving off the effects of...isolation, it is only a matter of time before it catches up with him*
>
> *(Wakefield 1980:28).*

Studies have revealed that reduced sensory input may result in brain inactivity. A reduction in sensory input through sensory restriction results in a significant reduction in mental alertness and poor concentration, a reduction in motivation and planning and also a reduction in the level of physical activity in motor systems and speech (Scott and Gendreau, 1969:338).

Inmates' Lack of Control

The high level of control over every area of the inmates' lives, or what is called "an authoritarian system of social control", is the third harmful aspect of inmate isolation (McCleery, 1961:272). While inmates in correctional facilities experience a certain level of increased watchfulness and control from the prison authorities, inmates in solitary confinement witness extreme control, and they have few ways they can exercise personal autonomy.

In most cases, they are totally dependent on correction officers for the provision of their basic needs. According to the results of various researchers that studied the socio-psychological aspects of a prolonged jail term in extremely controlled facilities, some psychological reactions that are close to insanity have been identified, and they include:

- Apathy
- Vagaries
- Hatred
- Nervous instability
- Listlessness (Sutherland and Cressey, 1955:473)

Reasons for Inmate Isolation

There are several official reasons why inmates are kept in isolation, whether in a designated segregation wing in a general correctional facility or in a designed free-standing isolation. Inmates could be isolated based on the following reasons:

Protection

The use of protective segregation is for detaining vulnerable inmates and separating them from other inmates in a general jail facility for their own safety. This could be due to a request by inmates or the discretion of the correction officer. Some inmates that are vulnerable in the correction facility include:

- Police informants
- Former police officers
- Former correction officers
- Sex offenders
- Debtors
- Inmates that could inflict harm on themselves
- Inmates that can be harmed by other inmates

There are facilities where these inmates are allowed to associate with each other, while for others, they remain isolated like those in punitive segregation.

Punishment

One of the reasons inmates are isolated is to punish them for their misconduct while they are in custody, and it is usually for a limited period of time. Segregation is regarded as the most severe kind of punishment for very serious jail offenses; inmates are not allowed to have many personal belongings like inmates in a normal prison location. Inmates under this form of confinement are allowed to leave their cell for solitary exercise that will last for an hour, and in some instances inmates are not allowed to see their family or go out for exercise.

Prison Management

Administrative segregation is an internal tool that is used for isolating inmates that have been regarded as disruptive, potentially dangerous and a major source of management problem. Gang members are good examples of inmates kept in solitary confinement. The main reason they are isolated is to reduce the rate of violence and maintain discipline and order in correctional facilities.

The isolation of inmates is usually executed through an internal prison process that is governed by administrative rules. While some correctional facilities offer inmates structured regimes which start with a strict confinement, then followed by gradually improved opportunities to communicate with other prisoners, others are strictly separated throughout the period of their sentence.

National Security

One of the reasons for the use of solitary confinement is the protection of national and public security, especially for inmates who have been convicted of politically motivated crimes and also prominent members of major criminal gangs. The aim of such confinement is to prevent the inmate from having contact with subversive groups, terrorists and organized crime gangs outside the jail facility. Another reason why inmates are placed in confinement is to prevent political inmates from releasing State secrets. Convicted inmates that have been isolated because they pose a threat to national security will most likely spend their jail sentence strictly in solitary confinement.

Pre-Charge and Pre-Trial Investigation

Suspects undergoing interrogation could be placed in isolation without being charged, although in some jurisdictions, such detention is limited to a few hours, while in others, it could last for a longer period of time. The reason for the isolation of suspects while they are being interrogated is to prevent them from compromising the investigation.

Lack of Correctional Facility Solutions

Sometimes, inmates are placed in solitary confinement due to the absence of proper alternatives for accommodating them. A good example will be inmates that are mentally ill; they can be isolated when there are no secure beds in the hospital. Most of the inmates may not pose problems to others or themselves, but they are prone to abuse and other inmates may be affected by their behavior. Inmates may be segregated when there is overcrowding while they await the proper space that will suit their classification to be made available.

Recommendations

In order to ensure that the isolation of inmates meets its intended purpose, whether as a punitive measure or a safeguard, the following tips should be considered when an inmate is being placed in solitary confinement:

- Inmates should be allowed to make representations on their case at a formal hearing
- The inmates should be informed of the reason why they are being segregated in writing

- The placement of the inmate should be constantly reviewed at short intervals
- When the isolation of the inmate is for punitive purposes, it must be used as a last resort and should not be allowed to last longer than a few days
- The prolonged isolation of inmates should only be used in the most extreme cases
- Mentally ill inmates must not be isolated
- Vocational and educational programs should be made available for inmates in solitary confinement
- Family members should be allowed to visit regularly
- Activities that brings inmates in contact with other inmates should be allowed where possible (Shalev, 2008)

Isolated inmates stay inside their cells for up to 24 hours a day, with limited contact with other people, with few ways and things to keep them busy while they are isolated in their cells. Prolonged isolation of inmates in such conditions can be mentally and physically taxing, but the effects of such confinement can be mitigated to a certain level when inmates placed in solitary confinement are accommodated in spacious cells that will enable them to carry out their daily activities in a humane environment. They should also have access to exercise and fresh air with a reasonable level of contact with other people, and they should be visited at least by their family members. Efforts should be made by jail administrators and staff to ensure that the harmful aspects of inmate isolation are greatly reduced and inmates are not kept in such confinement for a prolonged period of time.

Summary

Most people outside the criminal justice community are presently unaware of the proliferation of ultra-maximum security "lockdown" units and highly secured prisons and jails located within prisons where inmates are incarcerated for 23 hours daily. The movement of the inmates is monitored by video surveillance, which is also assisted by electronic door systems. These maximum security units, cameras, special alarms, and security devices are installed everywhere to control the movement of inmates and their actions. The living conditions of inmates in these maximum security units is extremely difficult, inmates experience an extraordinary degree of idleness, which happens to be one of the most difficult aspects of life in solitary confinement.

After the evaluation of over 100 inmates in federal and state prisons by Dr. Stuart Grassian, who is a psychiatrist, he concluded that the lockdown of inmates can cause symptoms like massive free-floating anxiety, perpetual distortions, and hallucinations, confused states, violent outbursts, delusional ideas, difficulties in thinking, panic attacks, overt paranoia and difficulty in concentration (Grassian, 2006).

Apart from affecting the inmates, the isolation of inmates also has social and environmental influences which are termed "social pathologies". It is defined as:

> *...adjustments in thinking, feeling, and behaving to adapt to Supermax conditions that can be long lasting, difficult to measure, and unknown even to the prisoner that make it possible to survive in isolation, but once released, set limits on what the person can become.*
>
> *(Haney, 2003 p. 138)*

Generally, released inmates may experience an institutionalization effect, where they may not be able to cope with the expectations and demands of society (Clements et al. 2007). Considering the fact that inmates in solitary confinement literally depend on the officers to dictate all their movements, this could lead to the loss of their ability to initiate or have a purpose in a broad range of behavior (Haney, 2009).

Psychologists have recommended the use of the assessment model in Supermax prisons which incorporates the severity of need through the use of standardized metrics rather than the use of clinical evaluation. In a situation where there are funding issues preventing the availability of a sufficient number of health practitioners from providing the necessary services, psychologists could actually work with corrections officers to utilize similar methods. When statistical formulas are used, the decisions to transfer offenders to solitary confinement would be done with less personal judgment and bias, although statistical predictions of inmate violence and suicide are never completely reliable (Adams and Ferrandino, 2008).

Other factors to consider include: reforming the criteria for sending inmates to solitary confinement, limiting the amount of time inmates can stay in isolation without subsequent psychological evaluation of the inmates and documented evidence why they should remain in isolation and also promoting the education of corrections officers about individual and environmental influences of mental illness. Several recommendations in the literature have been made on three levels of impact: prison staff, individual inmates and the role of Supermaxes within prisons or solitary confinement. Psychologists can advocate implementing routine standardized assessments in order to help determine accurately if the future risk and appropriate treatment needs are all practical solutions to the challenges associated with long-term isolation of inmates in prisons (Ceresnie, A. 2009).

Keywords: Confinement, Isolation, Solitary, Safeguard, Inmates, Incarceration, Prisoner.

CHAPTER ELEVEN

Effective Ways to Prepare for a Correctional Audit

The function of a correctional audit is to ascertain if a correctional facility is complying with the established performance indicators, policies or standards. These performance indicators could be mandated by the legislature or standards needed by an accreditation body like the ACA, and the performance indicators could also be the requirements that were set by the correctional facility itself. The audit of the correctional facility can be done either by an external entity or by internal auditing mechanism, audits could be a simple paper review which will involve a checklist or a complex audit that needs to be done before a facility can be accredited (Deitch, 2006).

Generally, the audit of the correctional facility provides the jail administrators or the regulatory bodies with an objective measure of the level of operation of the facility. Usually, It is used to confirm if the taxpayer's monies are judiciously utilized. There is emphasis on audit as a management tool which tends to provide answers to salient questions such as:

- Are corrections officers abiding by the established standards and policies?
- Does any gap exists between the policy and the practice?
- Are there changes in statistics, and if there are changes, why?

The answer to these questions and more will help the jail administrator with valuable information needed for a proactive and effective prison management (Deitch, 2006).

Preparing in Advance for Correctional Facility Audit

One of the best ways to have a successful audit is to listen to the suggestions that are offered by auditors during the inspection. When jail administrators prepare the facility properly for an audit, the audit will be easier, faster and in a more relaxed atmosphere. The following tips will be useful in proper preparation for an audit exercise:

- Prison administrators need to delegate tasks directly to different categories of corrections officers and also involve them in the audit preparation. All assignments should last through the audit in order to foster consistency.
- There is a need to individually review the standards by administrators, and they should also refer to the standards manual to ensure proper understanding of the compliance and criteria explanation.
- To ensure a successful audit, jail administrators need to designate an audit coordinator to supervise the entire operation and also provide periodic reports to the managing official. Authority should be given to the audit coordinator so as to provide access to other correction officers and even officers of higher ranks in order to have a proper documentation that is required.
- The policies and procedures need to comply with the standard requirements. This means that there may be a need to revise the procedure and policy of the facility if there are discrepancies. In a situation where administrators are not sure if their policies and procedures will comply with the standard requirement, the inspection team can be contacted to help review them before the implementation. There should be a routine assessment of facility procedures and policies against the actual documentation and practice.
- In order to effectively monitor all functions that need to be executed, a tickler system should be developed. This system will ensure that the performed functions are documented at specific frequencies which could be weekly, monthly, yearly, etc. This process is a great way to meet up with other regulatory agency inspections, such as health, menu approval, fire and others.
- There should be proper maintenance repair of the physical plant to ensure that they are functioning at their best all the time (MCCS).

Getting Set for Inspection Day

When the day for the inspection has been fixed, the following tips will help administrators to ensure a smooth inspection of the facility.

Physical Plant Inspection

Jail administrators need to personally walk through the correctional facility to inspect the physical plant in order to ensure that it is in a condition that the audit team will be comfortable with. Other things to inspect before the audit team comes include:

- Lighting
- Extinguishers
- Annunciator boards
- Smoke detectors
- Posted exits
- Excess inmate property
- Sanitary laundry procedures
- Corrections staff appearance
- Maintenance repair issues
- Inmate order
- Security breach

There is a need to advise all line staff and supervisory officers of the dates for the audit and also the purpose of the audit. It is most likely that involved corrections officers who know the reason for the inspection will take pride in executing their job. The audit process section of the standards manual needs to be reviewed to provide a clue as to what is expected of the facility. The review of the documentation can be done in a private area like a conference room.

Tour Guides

Jail administrators should designate competent tour guides ahead of the inspection of the facility. The corrections officers to be appointed should be very familiar with the layout of the correctional facility and will be able to move through every part of the facility without stress. Every means of access and keys that will be used need to be checked and made available to the escorts. The tour is usually split into two when the correctional facility is a large one, and two separate teams of auditors will inspect the facility. This will also require two teams of escorts to guide the auditors separately. Every logistics has to be worked out ahead of time, and a practice can be done in order to identify and resolve potential problems (MCCS).

Employee Data

The documentation that will show compliance with standards requiring corrections officers' awareness and training should be presented separately from other information, and formal training, whether in-service or pre-service, is acceptable. An updated employee roster has to be prepared, and it should include the names, date of employment and positions of employees. Volunteers and contractual employees should also be included. A summary documentation will make the auditing process for the training-related standards faster.

Conducting Self-Audit

In order to ensure adequate preparation for the audit, correctional facilities need to carry out periodic self-audit by making use of the standard worksheets as their guide. This prepares the facility ahead for external audit without many issues. There is a need to network with other managing officials, and the pre-audits have to be carried out at least six months before the actual audit. By carrying out the self-audit early, administrators will be able to make the necessary adjustments in order to be fully ready for the main inspection. A crucial type of audit that correctional facilities conduct internally is the emergency preparedness audit. It is an audit that helps to determine the level of preparedness of the institution in the event of major crises such as natural disasters, fire and inmate violence.

Benefits of Emergency Preparedness Audit

Conducting an emergency preparedness audit has several benefits to the corrections administrators, officers, and inmates. The benefits include:

- It provides the jail administrators with an objective assessment of the status and progress of the emergency system, considering the large and multifaceted nature of the prison emergency system. A systemic audit procedure will be able to evaluate the system effectively.
- An emergency preparedness audit helps to validate a comprehensive emergency preparedness system due to the fact that preparedness

for major emergencies, crises, and natural disasters is not an easy task.

- It provides the administrators with the information needed to identify traits of complacency and cutting corners in critical practices. It helps leaders to reduce the rate of turnover in supervisory and management positions, which leads to the loss of experience and knowledge in vital areas.
- An emergency preparedness audit helps to confirm that the correction staff is complying with standards and policies (Schwartz et al. 2009).

Who Conducts The Self-Audit?

It is better that a team is mandated to conduct the internal audit rather than an individual; more officers will develop an interest in the task and take ownership of the jail's emergency preparedness. Also, the correctional facility will benefit more from assessments made by two or more officers, which will likely expose the problems that an officer may not easily see. An ideal audit team should have at least two or more members, with a member appointed as the leader. The input of an officer that has served as an emergency preparedness coordinator will also be useful in the team (Schwartz et al. 2009).

Standards for Auditors

The audit team for the emergency preparedness needs to be guided by basic standards to enable them to perform their duties professionally and effectively. Some of the standards include:

- **The auditors should maintain confidentiality** - The information and findings of the audit team is confidential, and therefore access to the findings should be given only to top jail administrators, who will then make a decision on how the information will be disseminated.
- **The audit team needs to be discreet** - When there is a finding which reveals a potential deficiency or problems in any area, they should not disclose it to jail officers unless they are asked. Discussion with staff while the audit is being conducted should be limited in order to prevent being asked many questions.
- **Dealing with dangerous situations** - When dangerous situations

such as a life-threatening situation have been noticed by the audit team, the prison administrator should be notified immediately.

- **They should be ethical** - The audit team should be ethical. Artificial conditions should not be created in order to detect deficiencies in practice; such situations could be hiding the keys left lying around or hiding documents to see how long it will take officers to notice the change. They need to use legitimate opportunities in their evaluation.
- **Avoid indicting individuals** - The team should try as much as possible to report their findings in a way that will not point at a particular officer, but in the event that the issue is as a result of ignorance to policy, cutting corners, complacency or any other violations of standard policy or practice, then auditors should make reference to the individuals involved to enable them to undergo training or supervision.
- **Professionalism** - The auditors should be professional. Their roles, findings or information should not be used to create dissension.
- **Rigorous audit** - The auditors should not assume that something is acceptable without verifying it. They should not ignore the problems they discover or give a passing mark to the facility on items that are obviously deficient.
- **The use of appropriate method** - The best method that the audit team can adopt is the direct observation of the practices; however, the combination of documents and observation during the audit process will ensure consistency of policy and practice.
- **Be objective** - The team of auditors should maintain professionalism and objectivity by focusing on the evaluation criteria, and not on their personal preferences (Schwartz et al. 2009).

Mock Audits

For accreditation purposes, the management of a correctional facility can request mock audits. The Standards and Accreditation Department will arrange for a complete audit team that will conduct the audit to check the readiness level of the correctional facility. The mock audit is aimed at assessing the level of compliance with the standards. The mock audit team will carry out the following activities:

- They will tour the correctional facility

- Corrections staff, inmates and others will be appropriately interviewed
- They will carry out an examination of the physical plant
- The team will review completed standards, compliance folders, files, and records
- A report will be prepared for the correctional facility which will contain their findings and may include recommendations that will facilitate standards compliance

By having a mock audit, correctional facilities will be able to know their areas of weaknesses that need improvement. Considering the fact that the mock audit was conducted by the accreditation department, the result of the audit will likely be a reflection of the expected level of the audit when the real audit will be done (ACA, 2014).

One of the best ways to prepare for an audit exercise is to first conduct a self-audit. By carrying out a self-audit, the jail administrators will be able to know the possible areas of deficiencies and strength. Self-audits should be conducted before the auditors come, in order to give room for resolution of outstanding issues and also improve on every other area.

Summary

The audit of correctional facilities provides several benefits to the correctional facilities. It provides the opportunity for the evaluation or the re-evaluation of resource allocation. When there are increased administrative costs, training costs, and other costs, administrators will need to justify the spending. By carrying out an audit, it ensures accountability and also ensures the effective use of resources. An audit also helps to ensure that the correctional facility is well prepared for emergencies and that all security equipment in the facility is effective.

By carrying out an audit, the jail administrator will be able to identify their areas of weakness and also areas where they need to increase and improve on their activities. It provides the management with an objective assessment of the progress and the status of the emergency system in place (Schwartz, 2005).

The preparation for a jail audit starts immediately after the last inspection. The managers of the institution should start by carrying out an appraisal of the suggestions that was made by the auditing team while they inspected the facility. By listening to their suggestions and recommendations, administrators will be able to know the areas where they need to work on before the next audit is scheduled. When managers of correctional facilities start preparing for the next audit early, they will be more relaxed when the next audit takes place, and most times, the audit will not last for a long time. The preparation for the audit should involve various categories of correctional officers who will help to ensure consistency while the audit takes place (MCCS).

When conducting a self-audit, the management of correctional facilities needs to take it seriously. Jail administrators need to emphasize that self-audits are designed to assist the correctional institution in evaluating the important areas, such as security and the emergency preparedness of the facility. They should use the audit as a source of constructive change, and not for criticism. The findings of the self-audit should be reviewed by top management of the institution as soon as the self-audit is finished (Schwartz, 2005).

In preparation for a PREA audit, managers of correctional facilities should check the National PREA Resource Center Audit to have a better understanding of the audit process and the audit instrument. The aim of PREA auditing is to check the correctional facility's level of compliance with the PREA standards. There is also a need for mock audits before the PREA audit takes place (NIC, 2013).

When the administrators of correctional institutions are notified of an audit, the list of the team that will assist the inspection team should be made available, and if there are issues that could affect the conduct of the audit, such information should be communicated to the auditors, especially regarding the date. Access to the relevant areas of the facility should be given to the audit team, and also a designated work site should be made available for the audit team (Adult Facility Security Audits, 2015).

Every documentation that is needed by the auditors should be made available before the auditors come, in order to reduce the time it will take the audit to be conducted. Such documents or the shortcuts to the documents should be placed in a single electronic folder. By checking on the previous audits, administrators should be able to have knowledge of areas that need to be audited. It is important to have a pre-meeting before the auditors come. The pre-meeting should involve the correctional officers that will assist the auditors and the administrators to ensure that all that is needed for a smooth audit has been provided (National Council of Nonprofits).

Keywords: Audit, Inspection, Auditors, Corrections, Prison, Procedures, Policy, Inspection, Classification, Inmate,

CHAPTER TWELVE

Effective Distributive and Procedural Justice

Distributive and procedural justice are two out of the three important dimensions of organizational justice. They have been observed to be important variables that are useful in shaping correctional staff, job stress, organizational commitment, and job satisfaction. Based on the results from a multivariate analysis of survey data from the correctional staff at a state prison, it was discovered that staff distributive and procedural justice perception had a remarkable relationship with a measure of life satisfaction.

Substantial financial resources are needed to successfully operate the U.S. correctional facilities. Over $30 billion is spent annually to accommodate about 1.5 million offenders, though more of the expense is spent on the staff of over 430,000 people. The correctional facility staff is the most valuable asset of the correctional facilities, and while the staff has a positive effect on the operations of correctional facilities, the work environment also affects the staff.

It is therefore important, to understand how to effectively provide a conducive working environment that will enhance employee performance in correctional facilities. Employees will develop positive feelings when they have a high perception of organizational justice, and if they have a low perception of organizational justice, it could lead to negative feelings, such as anger, resentment, and frustration.

(Cropanzano, Goldman, & Benson, 2005; Judge & Colquitt, 2004; Lind & Tyler, 1988; Lucas, 2009)

Components of Organizational Justice

Organizational justice is comprised of three factors: distributive justice, procedural justice and a third one which is interactional justice. The employee perception of organizational justice is a major discovery that will help administrators in decision-making, because based on research, it could be beneficial when positively used or counterproductive when wrongly perceived. Attitudinal results from organizational justice could be:

- Leadership
- Organizational citizenship
- Turnover
- Job satisfaction
- Organizational commitment
- Trust
- Employee theft
- Job performance
- Customer satisfaction
- Alienation

(Cohen-Charash & Spector, 2001)

It was discovered that employees tend to develop and maintain a communal relationship with the company when they perceive that they were fairly treated by their company, and they are certainly going to be satisfied and more dedicated to their job than when they feel unfairly treated (Kim, 2009).

What is Distributive Justice?

Distributive justice is directly involved with several organizational outcomes, which include performance evaluations, a fair and just evaluation that will represent the actual employee efforts and work inputs in an organization. It has been identified that the perception of what is fair and what should be fair is part of the cognitive effects which determine the behavior and attitude of individuals at work (Lind, et al. 1997).

Basically, distributive justice is regarded as the individual's assessment of how well he/she is being treated in an organization. When defining distributive justice in an organization such as a correctional facility, it deals with the perception that there is a fair and equitable distribution of organizational outcomes which affect employees. This perception of distributive justice is basically centered on the "exchange principle", and when this principle is understood, employees will have a better feeling of justice.

The exchange principle is a concept which has to do with employee evaluation of organizational outputs which they received in comparison with employee input. The aim of the evaluation is to determine the fairness of the outcome (Lambert, 2003). There are several outcomes that are involved in employee perception process, such as:

- Evaluations
- Assignments
- Rewards and motivations
- Pay
- Performance
- Punishment

(Greenberg, 1990a, 1990b)

Distributive Norms

According to the definition of Forsyth, there are five types of distributive norms:

- **Equity** - This implies that members' outcomes should be based on their inputs. Employees that invest more time, money or energy should get more than those who contributed less.
- **Power** - Those who have more status, authority or control over the group should get more than employees in lower positions.
- **Equality** - All members of the group should have equal share, regardless of their contribution.
- **Responsibility** - Members of the group with more resources should share with those who have less.
- **Need** - Individuals with more needs should be given more resources than those who already have them, despite the level of their contribution.

(Forsyth D. R, 2006)

Outcomes of Distributive Justice

There are several outcomes or effects of distributive justice on the employee. It has an effect on employee performance when productivity and efficiency are involved (Cohen-Charash & Spector, 2001). There is an increase in employee performance with improved employee perception of justice (Karriker & Williams, 2009). Organizational citizenship behaviors refer to employee actions which are in support of the organization, even though it falls outside the scope of their job description. This employee behavior is greatly dependent on the extent to which staff views the organization as distributively just (Cohen-Charash & Spector, 2001).

Perceived Organizational Justice

Several studies have been conducted to ascertain the relationship between perceived organizational justice, organizational commitment, and job satisfaction. The results obtained from the study reveals that organizational justice which includes interactional justice, distributive justice, and procedural justice plays a crucial role in the development of organizational commitment and job satisfaction in employees. When employees perceive justice in the organization, they tend to have a higher feeling of satisfaction with their job, they are more committed and are less likely to quit their job.

Administrators and policy makers are therefore provided with insights into the relationship between employee perception of organizational justice and work attitudes. It will help them manage their employees better by using organizational justice perspective to attract positive behavioral response from their employees. This will provide several benefits to employees, listed below:

- It will enable administrators to have a better understanding on how to retain their valuable employees
- Administrators will be able to increase the commitment of valuable employees to their work and also help them derive satisfaction from their work
- It will also help them learn how to improve the performance of the employees and reduce employee turnover

Procedural Justice

Procedural justice is basically concerned with the judgment or perceptions of the employee regarding the process by which the allocation of decisions is made. Leventhal and colleagues have been given credit for extending procedural justice to organizational settings (Leventhal, et al.

1980). They emphasized six criteria which a procedure should meet in order to be regarded as fair:

- The procedure should be free from bias, which means that there is no third party with a vested interest in a specific settlement
- It should be applied across people and across time consistently
- The decision-making process should ensure the collection and use of accurate information
- A proper mechanism to correct inaccurate or unjust decisions should be provided
- The procedures should abide by individual or prevailing standards of ethics or morality
- The opinions of various groups that were affected by the procedure have been taken into account

Procedural justice encompasses a wide array of organizational procedures that are used to arrive at important organizational outcomes, like procedures for promotion, which has so much effect on employees (Lambert, 2003; Robbins, Summers, Miller, & Hendrix, 2000).

Models of Procedural Justice

There are so many views about what makes a procedure fair. The theory of procedural justice is indeed controversial; however, traditionally, these views are classified into three families:

- The Outcomes Model
- The Balancing Model
- The Participation Model
- Due Process and Natural Justice

The concept of procedural justice is quite influential in the law. In the U.S., for example, it reflects in the due process clauses of the United States Constitution and is commonly regarded as natural justice in other nations globally.

https://en.wikipedia.org/wiki/Procedural_justice

Interactional Justice

The third factor or component of organizational justice is interactional justice, and it relates to the treatment an employee gets when decisions are made. It can be promoted through the provision of explanations for decisions and disseminating the news in a sensitive and respectful manner (Bies & Moag, 1986). (Colquitt, et al. 2001) also suggested that interactional justice should be further divided into two components:

- Interpersonal justice
- Informational justice

The perception of respect and propriety in an individual's treatment is interpersonal justice, while informational justice refers to the provision of adequate explanation given in terms of truthfulness, specificity, and timeliness.

Effects of Distributive Justice and Procedural Justice on Staff Satisfaction

Based on the results of the survey of correctional staff, several effects of organizational justice among the staff were discovered: it was identified that correctional staff's perception of both distributive justice and procedural justice is related positively to their satisfaction with life, which gives credence to the contention that work activities affect every area of life of the staff.

Their belief that organizational justice exists in their workplace gives them more positive feeling or state of mind towards their work and less stress, and this leads to a greater satisfaction with life. Staff perception of a low organizational fairness may likely lead staff to different negative states of mind, such as anger, frustration, and resentment; this gives the staff strain and stress in life, leading to a lack of satisfaction with life generally (Lambert, et al. 2011).

Summary

The daily activities and events that take place at the place of work greatly affect every aspect of the lives of employees in an organization. The feeling of organizational justice by staff members most likely gives them a more positive feeling towards work and reduces work stress, which enhances greater life satisfaction. The correctional facilities should be able to ensure that staff members have a positive perception of organizational justice which encompasses distributive, procedural and interactional justice.

It is obvious based on several studies conducted that organizational justice is undoubtedly at the heart of the legitimacy of an organization. Individuals will find it difficult to work for an organization they perceive as unjust, unfair, without integrity, and even when they work in such an organization, it could result in a lower quality of life.

(Greenberg, 1990b; Lincoln & Kalleberg, 1990; Taxman & Gordon, 2009)

The Correctional institution is a major aspect of the U.S. criminal justice system, and incredible sums of money are being spent yearly, almost 40 billion dollars annually, in order to accommodate and rehabilitate inmates and employ over 400,000 corrections officers (Pastore and Maguire, 2007). The staff of correctional institutions constitute an essential part of the institution, and they should be fairly treated in order to ensure effective service delivery. Procedural and distributive justice are two dimensions of organizational justice, and there is sufficient evidence to suggest that what happens at work can affect every aspect of the lives of corrections officers. The perception by correctional officers that there is organizational justice enables them to develop more positive feelings towards their work and stress, and this will lead to greater life satisfaction.

Also, the perception of a low organizational fairness can possibly lead to anger, frustration, and resentment, which will cause strain and stress in the lives of officers and lead to a decreased satisfaction with life generally. It is difficult to work for an organization that is perceived to be unjust, unfair and without integrity; doing so may likely result in negative emotions that lower the quality of life (Lambert, et al. 2011).

Although there are different dimensions to organizational justice, the two most important dimensions of organizational justice are procedural and distributive justice. Distributive justice emphasizes the perception of fairness of outcomes for employees in an organization, and it is based on the idea of equity. Distributive justice is also based on the exchange principle where people look at the work they have done in exchange for what they receive (Lambert, 2003, p. 157).

Procedural justice relates to the measure of fairness in the process that resolves disputes in correctional institutions and other organizations and also the fairness with which resources were allocated. Procedural justice is crucial in dealing with corrections officers and also inmates; a fair and humane treatment of inmates greatly enhances the well-being of inmates and is generally acclaimed to reduce inmates' psychological distress, misconduct in correctional facilities and also their criminal behavior after they are released from the correctional institution.

Results from multilevel analyses reveal that inmates perceived their treatment in jail as more procedurally just in units where there were more female officers and also where officers have a more positive attitude towards the inmate rehabilitation and where there is a higher staff-to-prisoner ratio (Beijersbergen, 2013).

Results from studies indicate that both procedural and distributive justice are correlated to important outcomes, not just for the correctional institutions, but also for the staff. The improvement of the individual's perception of organizational justice lessens administrative implications and also promotes a positive environment for correctional organizations and employees. Life satisfaction is a cognitive assessment by an individual regarding the overall level of satisfaction with his/her life; it basically relates to the level of an individual's satisfaction and happiness with life generally and an assessment of the quality of life a person feels he or she has. When people are happier, they have the tendency to be more open-minded and also creative in their thinking, and they tend to exhibit rigid thinking and tunnel vision when they are dissatisfied, unhappy and stressful (Donovan, et al. 2002).

CHAPTER THIRTEEN

Effective Ways to Recruit and Rehire Valuable Employees

Obviously, one of the most challenging issues that correctional facility administrators face presently is the need to attract and also retain adequate numbers of high-quality officers. As a result of the challenge of hiring correctional officers, jail administrators have examined the connection between their organizations and the local labor environment. During the recruitment process, the defining elements of an agency include: the method of jail supervision, resources, and size intersect with local factors, especially the local economy and demographics. This intersection provides opportunities and also obstacles, and many administrators have devised ways of avoiding the disadvantages while taking advantage of the merits within their organizations (Clem, et al. 2000).

There has been a steady increase in the attention that is given to employee recruitment by researchers in recent years (Billsberry, 2007; Breaugh, et al. 2008). The importance of the recruitment process to every organization justifies the level of attention the topic is attracting, and the level of organizational growth in any organization greatly depends on the quality of the employees.

Employees provide values and perspectives and attributes to organizational life, and these human traits, when effectively managed, will provide great benefits to the organization. Employee recruitment refers to the process of identification and attraction of potential candidates, both within and outside the organization, and the evaluation of the candidates for future employment. When the perfect candidates are identified, then the selection process begins.

Regarding the relative importance of recruitment in relation to the characteristics of a position, what is more important to job applicants includes several attributes of the position, such as the work hours, salary, and job task. Other recruitment variables, such as the company's website design, job advertisement and the behavior of the recruiter, attract less attention of job applicants (Rynes and Cable, 2003).

The Challenges of Effective Recruitment in Correctional Facilities

The obstacles that jail administrators encounter when recruiting competent candidates as correctional officers could be both internal and external. Several factors have been identified by jail administrators as the reason why it is difficult to attract the right candidates (Clem et al. 2000).

A Good Local Economy

As a result of the strong economy in local communities, there is a low level of unemployment, which causes jail administrators to compete with private organizations and public agencies for job applicants. Some of these organizations offer a better working condition for job applicants.

Competing With Law Enforcement

Correctional facilities have always been at a disadvantage when competing with law enforcement agencies for officers. Results from surveys reveal that many applicants for the position of the correctional officer are basically interested in law enforcement jobs. The primary reason for this interest is that patrol officers are paid more than correctional officers (Clem, et al. 2000).

Perceived Working Conditions

The perception of correctional facilities by the public is based on what the television reports. According to Linda Hawkins, she encountered potential applicants who think they will be exposed to sexual assault, and correctional officers are sadistic or just security guards. She is the manager of the Recruitment and Background Unit in the Multnomah County Sheriff's Office in Portland Oregon. Jail administrators also experience difficulty in getting qualified applicants for staff diversity.

Common Challenges with Applicants

Based on the outcome of research (Breaugh, et al. 2008; Rynes, et al. 2003), it has been discovered that applicants face several issues when applying for a job:

- Applicants are not very sure of what they want from the job they are applying for
- Most times, their understanding of what is involved in the position they are applying for is inaccurate and/or incomplete
- They lack self-insight in terms of their skills, knowledge, and abilities
- Job applicants are unable to predict accurately their response to the demands of a new position

Having an understanding of the challenges most job applicants face will help every organization to properly assist the job applicants. This can be in the form of clear and proper training of applicants to enable them to understand their roles and duties and the potentials in working with the organization.

Effective Recruitment Approaches for Correctional Facilities

There are several recruitment channels that correctional facilities use in recruiting officer. These vehicles ranges from outreach tools to community networks and also the current staff. Based on the results of a survey, the following were identified as effective approaches (Clem, et al. 2000).

Good Community Network

Every correctional facility belongs to a larger community, and when jail administrators create a cordial and favorable public perception of the correctional facility, it enhances the recruitment strength of correctional facilities. This favorable perception can be promoted through the following means:

- Partnering with local job services and also other agencies in advertising job openings
- Fostering greater community relations by educating the community about the real picture of correctional facilities in terms of the environment, operations, mission, and role

The Use of Outreach Tools

Correctional facilities can get their message across to potential officers by using several multimedia channels, such as:

- Placing advertisements in national and local publications
- The use of multimedia recruitment tools
- The Internet, by using a website which provides a great marketing opportunity for correctional facilities
- The use of job fairs is a traditional approach for recruitment; although it may not yield immediate results, it will serve as a seed or investment that will yield much later

Current Staff

Results from a survey of jail managers disclosed that current correctional officers are actually one of the best assets for recruitment. Several approaches have been employed in encouraging jail staff to help in maintaining an effective workforce (Clem, et al. 2000).

- **Informal Staff Involvement Approach** - This approach encourages jail staff to promote the correctional facility as a great place to work and inform applicants of job openings.
- **Formal Programs** - A formal program is an approach that provides training for volunteers from the current jail staff who are interested in executing specific recruitment tasks.
- **Incentive Reward Approach** - Some correctional facilities provide rewards to encourage more correctional officers to get involved in the recruitment exercise.

Effective Retention Tools

Employee retention in correctional facilities is very important, considering the challenges faced in employing new jail staff. Every prison administrator should engage in several strategies for staff retention.

- **Increased Pay** - It is obvious that with increase in pay, correctional facilities will be able to retain current staff. Jail administrators need to provide periodic pay adjustment as incentive and also overtime compensations.
- **Additional benefits** - The addition of extra benefits, such as fitness

facilities, public transportation subsidies, and others, will help to retain current staff.

Awards and Incentives

This could be in the form of a recognition for extra effort or unusual service, and such incentives and awards can motivate prison staff to stay and increase their productivity. The awards can be the "Employee of the Week" or a profound acknowledgment of the contribution of the officer (Clem et al. 2000).

Facility Assessment

In a bid to retain their valuable employees, many correctional facilities have imbibed the practice in private business which is aimed at obtaining information from their employees, which include those leaving. The information obtained by jail administrators will be used in making decisions that will ensure better working conditions.

Departing Employee

The correctional organization can obtain very useful information that is confidential from employees that are leaving. Such interviews will help to understand the reason why a correctional officer is leaving, and this will enable the jail administrator to find better ways of resolving such issues.

Internal Employee Survey

Apart from obtaining useful information from employees that are leaving the job, current staff members can also offer useful information that is confidential. The information will provide what is an ideal job expectation of the employees, and it could be formal or informal. Jail administrators can use the results of the survey as a guide to effective working conditions that will meet the expectation of the employees, which will help in the retention of current employees (Clem, et al. 2000).

Cost Implication of Hiring New Employees

Apart from the implementation of organizational policies that will benefit employees, it is perhaps more important that employers maintain a stable workforce. In order to maintain a stable workforce, employee turnover should be reduced by providing flexible workplace policies and better benefits. This will lead to the retention of employees which will save costs remarkably for employers. Replacing workers is costly; it could lead to productivity losses because someone will leave his/her job. Among the costs to be incurred when replacing employees include:

- The cost of hiring, which includes the cost of interviews
- Severance pay and also paying for temporary cover of an employee's duties, like overtime for other employees
- Advertisement costs, agency fees and expenses incurred in the screening of applicants, such as drug tests and background verification
- There will be lost clients in some instances and also lost institutional knowledge
- The cost of training new employees, like orientation, certifications, classroom training and on-the-job training
- Decrease in productivity pending when the new employee fully understands the new job

(Boushey, et al. 2012)

Effective Recruitment Model Steps

There are several models of recruitment: however, a close look at the recruitment research offered by (Breaugh et.al, 2008) reveals a thorough recruitment model that will be effective in the recruitment process. The first step involves the objective of the recruitment exercise; the answers to all other questions and outcomes must be consistent with the objectives of the recruitment.

Step One: Recruitment Aims

What are the recruitment objectives of the organization? This will serve as a blueprint or a guide in the recruitment process. The aims and objectives of the organization will help in eliminating candidates that are not qualified. The recruitment objectives include the following points:

- The type of applicant the organization is looking for, their education, work experience, interest, knowledge, ability, skills, and diversity.
- What is the time required to fill the position?
- The number of applicants needed
- What is the new hire retention rate?

- The job performance of the newly recruited employees
- The job satisfaction of new employees

Step Two: Development of Strategy

Every organization needs to develop a strategy that will help them in the recruitment process. Some of the factors to consider when developing a strategy include:

- Strategies to help reach the targeted people
- The ideal individual to recruit
- Where will the recruitment be?
- What is the timing of the recruitment activities?
- What is the message that will be communicated to attract the right applicants?
- Who should be chosen to act as the recruiter?
- What is the nature of site visit?
- The strategy will also include budget considerations
- The nature of the job offer is also important

Step Three: The Recruitment Activities

This step includes the proper recruitment activities, such as:

- The recruitment methods applied
- The features of information conveyed; timeliness, completeness, and realism
- Recruiters used for the recruitment process
- The hosting of the site visit
- Extension of the job offer

The Recruitment Results

The final stage of the recruitment process is the evaluation of the recruitment results. In order to select the best applicant in line with the organization's objective, employers need to compare their recruitment objectives against the outcomes of the recruitment (what was really accomplished after the process). This process enables employers to assess their performance and learn from the experience, which will lead to a more effective recruitment process (Breaugh, 2008).

The Realistic Job Previews

The use of Realistic job preview is based on a basic premise that most job applicants' perception of the positions they are applying for is inaccurate. Despite the fact that many employers endeavor to present their organization as a great place for anyone to work, the expectations of the applicants are generally inflated (Billsberry, 2007). Individuals that have an inflated job expectation are prone to be dissatisfied with their positions and may likely quit when compared to applicants that have a more accurate expectation (Breaugh and Starke, 2000).

In order to deal with the issue of inaccurate job expectations, employers should endeavor to provide candid information regarding the job, which includes the negative and positive attributes of the organization. This information can be provided by using booklets or videos (Phillips, 1998). When job applicants accept to stay after going through the Realistic job previews, then they will have what they expected, and this will result in several positive outcomes, such as employee retention, satisfaction and a sense of trust, because the organization was honest during the process of recruitment.

Summary

The United States in 2008 had about 16,000 general purpose state and local law enforcement agencies, and this includes the sheriff's office, the police department and 50 other primary state agencies. These agencies employed about 705,000 full-time sworn personnel. Although in 2008, the agencies hired about 61,000 officers; about 51,000 officers were lost through retirements, resignations and other types of separation.

Several recruitment methods have been used by different agencies for recruiting officers, and some of the methods include the use of websites, personal contacts, employment websites, newspapers, job fairs and special agents. There are several incentives that many law enforcement agencies provide to attract the right applicants for sworn positions, and one of such incentives is the provision of financial support to eliminate the cost of recruit training (Reaves, 2012).

Correctional agencies are presently faced with the formidable challenge of having to balance the increasing caseloads with the stagnant resources and more dangerous inmates. The agencies are expected to also be responsive to the escalating expectations and the changing public policies. The effectiveness of the solutions to these challenges depends on how present day leaders effectively develop tomorrow's workforce.

The ability of correctional agencies to positively contribute to public safety greatly depends on its workforce. Progressive correctional agencies need to be ready and plan for the retirement of Baby Boomers, the changing nature of the labor market and also the stiff competition for talented employees. Previously, competent employees competed for jobs; however, recent trends indicate that employers are in competition for competent and qualified applicants, which has created what is known as the "war for talent".

> *One in five Americans will be a senior citizen by 2030, compared with one in eight in the mid-1990s.*
>
> *(Arthur, 2001: 334)*

There is therefore, a great need to recruit and retain employees with very strong analytical, communication, problem-solving and collaborative skills in order to be able to implement concepts like evidence-based practices. Considering the fact that there will likely be a high employee turnover at the entry level, many corrections agencies that engage in strategic planning have a supply of qualified applicants that have been screened, tested and are ready to be hired within a relatively short notice. Although it takes years for employees to develop the level of competencies that is needed for effective supervision of inmates, corrections agencies need to be proactive in forecasting vacancies and the recruitment and training of officers to fill the available vacancies (Stinchcomb, et al. 2006).

There are several strategies that law enforcement agencies have adopted in retaining their officers. Some agencies required officers to sign a minimum time-of-service agreement with them, and many agencies opted for a 2-year term. Other retention strategies adopted by agencies includes: increased pay at specific milestones or take-home vehicles for officers, financial allowance for uniform-related expenses or free uniforms, and some agencies offered a pay raise for a college degree. Correctional agencies should adopt a strategy that works best for their needs in order to retain competent officers and reduce the rate of employee turnover.

One of the best recruitment tools for organizations is a positive image which creates the impression of a good place of work, and the recruitment of officers from a wide variety of generations also requires a wide variety of recruitment strategies and organizational incentives. The use of internships provides a win-win strategy for the correctional agency and the employee. It enables the agency to test the abilities of the intern without making a decision to hire while the intern gets an experience of the agency without making any employment commitment. Employee referrals are also a reliable strategy used in the recruitment of officers. Such referrals have been associated with financial incentives, but care should be taken if it concerns demographic balance of the current staff based on age, gender, culture or ethnicity (Reaves, 2012).

Keywords: Recruitment, Retain, Employees, Recruiter, Job Applicant, Correctional Facility, Correctional Officers, Recruit, Advertisement, Job Satisfaction, Interview.

CHAPTER FOUTEEN

Effective Methods to Prepare for Career Advancements

The word career advancement is a relative term. While for some individuals it implies climbing up the organizational ladder until there is no more room to climb or the employee reaches the top relative to the field of expertise of the employee, for others it could be an increase in salary scale, even if the employee will have to move from one organization to another. One of the important elements of employee satisfaction and retention in any organization is career advancement.

> *Clear opportunities for career advancement are an "especially powerful" employee motivator.*
>
> *Victor Lipman of Forbes*

Lipman observed that employees tended to be more motivated when their career paths are clear with specific goals to work towards, while they also feel less focused and less motivated when their career paths were non-existent or dim. The prospect of career advancement can motivate the staff of an organization to work hard (Brevis, et al. 2007: 399). Employees look forward to steady progress in the organization where they work (Mullins, 2007).

Career Advancement and Employee Turnover

From a theoretical point of view, the availability of opportunities for career advancement can greatly reduce the level of employee turnover, and lack of career advancement opportunities is a major driving force that can cause an employee to quit the job. Individuals that have been provided with more opportunities in their current organization will have fewer reasons why they want to leave. The cost of recruitment of new and competent employees to replace the jobs is high when compared to the cost of creating career opportunities (March et al. 1958).

Benefits of Career Advancement

The lack of advancement may likely hinder a manager's chance to climb the organizational ladder (Saari and Judge, 2004). The benefits of career advancement include:

- It provides employees with the chance to go through training and further their education
- It helps to groom a motivated workforce, which also leads to higher productivity
- It ensures job security for employees
- It also leads to job satisfaction
- Increased salary and long-term success

Career advancement provides great benefits both to the employee and also to the organization. While it gives employees the hope of better working conditions and pay, it also helps them focus on increasing their productivity, which is a benefit to the organization.

Essential Components of an Effective Career Plan

There are several aspects of the workplace that the management of an organization can address in order to increase the opportunities for advancement, engagement, and loyalty of employees. Some of these components include:

- Providing them with additional responsibilities that will lead to a change in their roles
- Provision of a well-planned career advancement program for each employee which aligns with their professional goals

- Acknowledgment of every employee's accomplishments through promotions and raises

Defining Your Career Advancement Priorities

There are several career advancement options available to employees, and it can be overwhelming to make a decision regarding where to focus on. Employees need to start with the basics, which include the talents and skills they love most and their values. How can employees access their career advancement opportunities? It is easy for employees to repeat the same mistakes; however, it is important that employees review their career history and seek the opportunities for improvement and identify pitfalls in order to avoid repeating them.

"Those who cannot remember the past are doomed to repeat it."

(Philosopher George Santayana)

Sponsorship

Although employers are involved in assisting employees in advancing their careers, the employees are also responsible for stating what they want to learn and achieve on their job and also actively pursue the knowledge and accomplishment independently of any development program from the employer. Employees can also get the chance to develop their skills for career advancement through sponsorship.

Sponsorship is a reciprocal relationship between the sponsor and the protégé. The sponsor will invest effort and time in enhancing and promoting their protégé's capabilities and also expect the employees being sponsored to increase their performance. The recipients of such endorsement need to put in more effort, and employees in need of sponsorship should find out how they can be valuable to the sponsor, and the sponsorship will flow (Sylvia Ann Hewlett). When searching for a sponsor, the employee needs to leave his or her comfort zone, have a clear dream and destination and be focused on the goal (Wrenn, 2013).

Training

Training is a very important factor that determines the extent to which an employee rises in an organization. Training involves the process of upgrading the knowledge and skills of the employee, which leads to an improvement in the employee's ability to perform tasks more efficiently. The training and development of employees in an organization is a critical factor. Considering the level of competition in the corporate world, it has become an issue of strategic importance ((Watts; Brevis, et al. 2007: 375).

By effectively training employees in an organization, organizational goals and values are directly transferred to the employees simultaneously. Training provides a benefit to the employee by increasing their knowledge and skill base, while also benefiting the organization by increasing their performance and productivity (Pillay et al. 2015).

Choosing a Learning Method

There are several avenues that are available for employees to train and develop themselves for career advancement. Employees need to access the options and make a choice that is most suitable for their career advancement goals. Some examples of programs that will provide training and education for employees include:

- **Formal Educational Programs** - There are several organizations that require formal degree certificates to achieve certain career goals. Employees can choose this option if it is required by their current organization or any other organization they intend to move to.
- **On-the-Job Training** - Organizations that require employees to have specific skills suited for their job can provide on-the-job training for employees; however, in the event that employees have not been provided with the opportunity to get the training, employees can request for a cross-train with a colleague or even offer to work for free in order to get the skills.
- **Self-Instruction** - It is also possible for individuals to acquire skills by buying materials that are related to the field they intend moving to (Piotrowski, 2009).

Create Opportunities for Continuous Learning

Sometimes, most organizations treat some positions statically, like the store manager position. When they do that, there is little or no room for advancement to the next position; rather, some organizations hire people from outside to fill the higher positions. This results in a high rate of employee turnover. Employees should be encouraged to engage in further education, which could be directly from the organization or from other professional development programs. Organizations need to enlighten their staff of the need for continuing their education, and those who further their education should be rewarded for the effort they made.

Encourage Innovation

Although large organizations may tend to create a special innovation team that will design and develop new products to grow the business or organization, it is essential that employees are provided with the opportunity to contribute their own creative ideas, and they should also be rewarded. This gives employees a stake in the organization and a long-term perspective. It also enhances their skills as they learn to take up new roles and responsibilities.

General Career Advancement Tips for Employees

- **Take on More Responsibilities** - One of the easiest ways to make career advancement is by taking on more responsibilities than what employees have been assigned to do. By asking for more responsibilities and effectively handling the extra responsibilities, employees become indispensable to the organization. It also connotes a deep interest and desire to help the department and the organization to attain their goals while adding value to the employment. Apart from the fact that the organization will appreciate every contribution to the success of the organization, their competitors will also recognize such employees, and a better deal will always be available.
- **Develop Effective Communication Skills** - It is common for ambitious professionals to find themselves out of their niche; however, in order to take advantage of such situations, employees should have good communication skills to enable them to fit into a wide range of roles that could arise due to career advancement. By having versatile communication skills, employees will be an asset that can translate knowledge across audiences, and such skills are difficult to outsource or replace.
- **Deal With Stress Gracefully** - Employees face stressful situations most times; however, addressing stressful situations provides employees with the opportunity to display one of the most valuable skills in the business and corporate world, which is the ability to stay cool and positive while dealing with setbacks without panicking. It is quite easy for people to notice such skills in employees who can thrive in almost any organization.

- **Simplify Complex Tasks** - As employees, one of the skills that will aid career advancement is the ability to simplify complex tasks. Simpler solutions are usually much easier to explain and roll out (Weiss, 2013).
- **Carefully Choose Necessary Qualifications** - Employees need to be strategic about the kind of training they intend to get, and it should align with their career goals. The following points can help employees to make the right choice of training and further education:
    - Employees need to check the job description of the position they desire to get, this could either be within the same organization or in another organization.
    - The use of a survey technique is also effective. Employees can carry out a survey of those already in the position they desire and ask relevant questions regarding their qualifications and the type of training they obtained.
    - By discovering what they lack, employees can improve on their weaknesses.

Build Diverse and Strong Professional Relationships

By building diverse and strong relationships, employees can advance their career in many powerful ways. It provides employees with a sufficient toolbox to handle projects, by making consultations with your contacts. Another benefit of having a good professional network is, in case an employee desires to make a career move, there will be sufficient references and professionals that will readily provide assistance (Piotrowski, 2009).

A strategic way to build a network is for employees to refine their personal brand, share information about their passion through social media, print media and at industry events. This will provide the opportunity to network with professionals in their field. In building the list of contacts, potential contacts can fall into different categories:

- **Related-Service Providers** - Contacts that fall under this category are individuals who are within the employee's organization that may be recruiters.
- **The Hub Contacts** - These are people whose work brings them in contact with people from different backgrounds, such as real estate, investment, and insurance.

- **Decision Makers** - They are individuals that have a direct say on the possibility of a career advancement in the organization, and employees can target such people in other organizations if they desire a move from their present organization.

Assessing Your Top Talents and Skills

Sometimes, people do not take note of their best talents and skills, although it is much easier for other people to clearly identify the strength and skill that employees use in their organization. It is recommended that employees should complete a standardized strengths or aptitude assessment in the course of their career to help them discover their unique talents that can be used for career advancement. The results of such tests will indicate areas of strength and weaknesses, and employees can make career decisions based on the results obtained.

Career Advancing Associations and Groups

Being part of a team that has a common goal is a powerful tool in achieving great goals, and the same applies to career advancement. By associating with a career advancing association, individuals can make progress faster, though the challenge mostly encountered is finding the right groups. In order to choose the right association, individuals need to consider those that are associated with their industry or specialty. Some organizations that employees can belong to that can help foster their career advancement include:

- **Civic Organizations** - Most civic organizations are locally based, and they focus on community development through volunteer and fundraising programs like a Rotary club. Such organizations provide a good platform to network and increase contact base.
- **Business Networking Groups** - This involves the groups that employees' present organization belong to, and any other organization that employees seek to move to. A good example of such groups is the Chamber of Commerce Organizations.
- **Professional Associations** - Most professionals seeking career advancement can easily increase the chance to achieve that goal by joining their professional associations. It also provides professionals with the current and best practices available in their industry. Employees seeking to climb the ladder in their current career will

have access to colleagues that can open new doors (Piotrowski, 2009).

Career advancement serves both the employee and the organization. While it provides employees with the prospect of a better position with increased pay and responsibilities, it also reduces the level of employee turnover, which saves the organization the extra cost required to recruit new workers. Organizations need to create the enabling environment for employee development through on-the-job training and also motivate and reward employees that make personal efforts towards their development.

Keywords: Advancement, Career, Organization, Training, Development, Ladder, Promotion, Sponsor, Employee, Corporate, Business

CHAPTER FIFTEEN
Effective Methods to Improve Employee Performance

The development of strategies that will help every employee in the organization to realize their potential is the role of human resources. The human resources management in an organization is saddled with the responsibility of understanding the potentials, motivations, and performances of employees. Every organization that desires to achieve great success in their field must know how to activate the full potentials of their employees (Boswell and Boudreau, 2000).

Performance can be defined as the accomplishment of an assigned task that will be measured against set standards, which include completeness, accuracy, speed and cost. The organizational performance also consists of the actual output of an organization or firm as measured against their target output, which could be their objectives or goals.

Available results from statistical indicators and several studies reveal that the competitiveness and success of organizations greatly depends on the professional performance of their employees, and strategies to help improve their success is a major concern in a competitive market (Campbell et al. 1998; Chen and Kuo, 2004).

Several companies have adopted the balanced scorecard methodology in managing organizational performance. With this method, performance can be monitored and measured in multiple dimensions, like:

- Customer service

- Organizational performance
- Employee stewardship
- Financial performance
- Social responsibility
- Performance measurement systems
- Organizational engineering (Richard et al. 2009)

Planning and Career Development of Employees

Transforming a job into a career for employees is one of the best strategies that can be adopted to ensure the commitment and loyalty of employees in the organization. By helping them understand that they have a future in the organization, they will devote their personal time to prepare for opportunities and a promotion that might take place (Harrington, 2001). Employees see career development as a guarantee for a position in the organization where they work. Although based on the results of a survey conducted, most managers regard career planning as a difficult task which is devoted exclusively to the interests of employees, and they do not see how it will benefit the organization; however, it provides benefits both to the employee and also the organization in several ways.

- It leads to an increase in employee satisfaction
- It lowers the cost of employee turnover for the organization
- It enhances employee loyalty to the organization
- Career development helps in attracting and also retaining performing employees
- It also increases employee performance
- Employees will have increased autonomy and responsibility
- It enhances the achievement of knowledge and experience (Chişu, 2002)

Contributions from other authors reveal that without career planning, organizations are at the risk of an error-prone, disappointed and underused workforce that will most likely migrate towards other organizations that will provide them with better working conditions (Harrington, 2001). Career planning will help to reduce the cost of the labor movement that is incurred by organizations and foster a greater level of loyalty from employees.

Employee Training and Development

Employee training, related to professional development, is a great strategy that organizations can adopt in enhancing employee performance (Bocean, 2009: 27). While training is the development of new capabilities, development involves improving existing employee capacities. The results of a study carried out by the Society for Human Resource Management shows that 40% of managers in organizations consider training employees as the most crucial function of human resource management (Konrad and Deckop, 2001).

Training is a great tool that is used to develop the knowledge and skills of employees, which will ultimately increase the employee's performance and also the organization's performance in terms of effectiveness, efficiency, and productivity. By training and motivating the employees, the downtime of the machinery will be minimized, since they will be able to easily diagnose and most likely repair any identified fault. The skills of employees will improve when they are properly trained, and they can help to improve the functional flexibility of the organization because they can be retrained, considering their broad knowledge of base multi-skills.

In the current intensified international competitive trend, efficient production, even though it is for technically unsophisticated products, benefits from a technically advanced machinery that is operated by employees with high level of skill, which will also become a pre-condition for the successful selection of the right machinery and its efficient utilization (Steedman and Wagner, 1989).

Employee Mentoring and Coaching

Managers and supervisors through the interactive process of coaching try to resolve issues that have to do with performance. They seek to develop employee capacity through collaboration based on three components: personal support, technical support and individual challenge (Luecke, 2004). The purpose of coaching is to enhance professional performance, unlock the potential in people so as to grant them the enablement to maximize their performance and correct behaviors that are inappropriate.

Employees are able to understand their limitations, which is the reason for their failures and low performance, through coaching. Coaching also assists employees to discover the causes that prevent progress in specific fields (Bocean, 2009). According to (Luecke, 2004), while coaching has to do with the current work and job, mentoring has to do with the career in general. Mentoring and coaching require efforts and daily interaction in the workplace between managers and subordinates.

Performance and Feedback Strategy

Several studies that researched on the effects of feedback on performance came to a conclusion that generally, individuals that get frequent and immediate feedback are able to achieve better performance than those who did not receive any (Stewart and Brown, 2011). The aim of feedback is to help determine the necessary actions that will help to improve performance which could be corrective, though the preventive action is more desirable.

Feedback is a crucial element of an employee's development and performance. Organizations need to determine, above all, if the aim of feedback is only for development, or if it will be evaluative and then linked to reward and promotion (Ratiu, et al, 2011). The reaction of some employees that get negative feedback initially will be to make greater efforts, while some will be demotivated and defensive.

In order to ensure that negative feedback leads to better performance, employees should be made to know that they possess the required skills to improve their performance in the future. Although many managers tend to avoid discussing negative aspects of employee assessment, it is not always the best, because employees may not be aware of their weaknesses and the consequences of their weaknesses. This provides the employee with little information that will be helpful in improving their performance (Ratiu, et al. 2010).

Effective Communication

Most employees desire to be a part of a compelling future and know the goals of their organization. Employees can get this information through the clear communication of goals and expectations of the organization. Managers need to inform them about the activities of the organization and let communication be truthful and hopeful, even though, managers may have to share bad news sometimes. In communicating bad news, it is important that you deliver the news strategically.

Another aspect of communication is an open channel of communication in the organization. Managers can understand what is important to the employee through surveys, team meetings, and suggestion boxes. It is important to encourage employees to express their perspectives and ideas without criticism, and the management should be ready to implement positive ideas and suggestions made by employees.

When their suggestions and complaints are properly addressed, employees are encouraged and they will have a sense of ownership. When employees hear of an important update of their organization from friends or the media, it could have a serious effect on the employee engagement. Managers should ensure that employees get any new updates about their organizations first before people outside the organization will hear.

Job Insecurity and Pay Strategy

This strategy is the same as the carrot and stick approach for employees. The use of pay in enhancing employee performance has been a long practice, and it has not always been successful to extract labor effort. Organizations may attract and retain their employees by giving them higher wages than the average rate in the labor market that is downwardly flexible. This approach, which is the carrot approach, can be reinforced by the stick, which is the introduction of a sense of job insecurity which could be through outsourcing. Efficiency and labor productivity can be achieved by a stable and hard-working workforce under the threat of job insecurity, and also, employee's flexibility and commitment can be secured by effectively playing the labor markets (Rubery, 1997).

Collaborate on Problem Solving

The sense of empowerment of employees will diminish when they have the belief that the leaders or managers are the ones who solve the problems. This ultimately decreases their engagement over time. Employees and team members should be encouraged to take responsibility and deal with issues collaboratively or individually, and they should not have the feeling that it is the manager's duty to fix everyone else's problems.

General Strategies to Improve Employee Performance

When employees are empowered, they are happy; and when they are happy, they become more productive. These general tips will be very useful in increasing the performance of employees in an organization:

- **Delegation** - By delegating tasks to employees, it increases their ownership of the task and shows that they are trusted to do the job properly.
- **Celebrate Their Achievements** - Employee achievements, whether

financial or non-financial, should be celebrated. It will serve as a motivation.

- **Develop Strong Teams** - Employees will perform better when they get along with other members of the team and also participate in a team environment.
- **Ask the Right Questions** - Managers need to ask employees the right questions. The questions should be open-ended and address the root cause of their problems. They should also be ready to listen attentively to understand what employees want.

Total Quality Management Approach

This approach originated from quality assurance methods which were adopted during World War I. It is a business approach that aims to provide quality products in order to achieve customer satisfaction. It has several foundations, which include:

- A proper and computerized procedural evaluation of the performance of employees regarding their output
- Employee accountability and responsibility on the job
- Organizational support for employees to enable them to work in teams
- Empowerment and involvement of employees in tasks
- The commitment of executive management to practice Total Quality Management Approach
- Decision-making based on the measurement of results (Gui et al. 2012)

The AACC Concept

Total Quality Management was linked with human resources in an article entitled "Total Quality Human Resources Management"-TQHRM, and the concept of AACC was explained this way:

- **Alignment-** Employees can achieve alignment and cohesion in their work when they understand the nature of the target market, business, shareholders, needs and customers' demands. A well-defined standard of operating procedures and policies will assist employees in achieving goals and tasks.
- **Authority** - Employees can be given authority and autonomy to be

able to meet quality in their work. There should not be a communication gap between the employer and employee.

- **Competencies and Capabilities of Employees** - Employees' competencies and capabilities should be enhanced by providing adequate training and development programs and opportunities.
- **Commitment and Retention** - The commitment of employees and their retention is crucial for regularity and uniformity in organization's operations. This can be attained through the acknowledgment and rewards of an employee's work.

(VanDevender, 2011)

The attainment of organizational goals and objectives can only be possible when they embark on strategies that will enhance the performance of their employees. Despite the fact that several authors may have different views regarding employee performance, most authors agree that the human resources management practices can enhance the performance of organizations by increasing the abilities and skills of employees, expanding the responsibilities of employees to enable them to utilize their abilities effectively, increase their motivation and promote positive attitudes (Patterson et al. 1997).

Keywords: Improvement, Mentoring, Motivation, Employee, Strategies, Performance, Productivity, Development, Training, competence, Reward, Improve, Strategies, Commitment, Communication.

CHAPTER SIXTEEN
Effective Correctional Rehabilitation That Works

Over seven million offenders undergo some form of correctional supervision in the United States daily, which is one in every 32 adults and approximately one-third of the incarcerated, while the remainder are either on probation or on parole (Glaze and Bonczar, 2006). It is also estimated that, out of the inmates incarcerated, approximately 600,000 are released to the community yearly (Hughes and Wilson, 2002; Travis, 2005).

Initially, most programs for offenders placed emphasis on religious instruction which was expected to help inmates attain spiritual enlightenment. Inmates were kept in solitary confinement to enable offenders realize their sinful ways and reflect on their criminal activities and repent (Gerber & Fritsch, 1995; Teeters, 1955). The focus on religious instruction was shifted gradually to the reformation era, where inmates were taught communication and basic literacy skills. Credit is usually given to Zebulon R. Brockway for initiating this era in 1876 when he proposed the rehabilitation theory at the first conference of the American Prison Association.

The reformatory era led to the rehabilitation era, where inmates are released when there is sufficient evidence to suggest that they have been effectively rehabilitated. The goal of the rehabilitation era is to correct through rehabilitation, and it was practiced until the 1970s, when the focus in the United States corrections changed from rehabilitation to crime control philosophies, which placed emphasis on incapacitation, retribution, and deterrence (MacKenzie, 2006).

The rehabilitation perspective works based on the assumption that the prison systems should not only seek to punish offenders for their crimes, but also reduce the crime rate and foster safer communities. In order to actualize the goal of rehabilitation of inmates, corrections officers should reduce the potential for inmates under their jurisdiction to reoffend when they are released from supervision or the correctional facility (Lipsey et al. 2007).

Reason for Inmates' Rehabilitation

Despite the fact that the application of the "tough on crime" method in deterring criminal activities has its advantages, the use of education and rehabilitation of inmates also has its merits. One of the reasons for the consistent emphasis on the education of inmates is that, there is a strong correlation between educational level and criminal activity. On average, convicted offenders have fewer job skills and less education than the general population (Andrews & Bonta, 2003; Harlow, 2003).

For instance, 41% of offenders in jail or prisons and 31% of probationers have not completed high school or its equivalent (Harlow, 2003). According to the U.S. Department of Education, the level of illiteracy of incarcerated adults is also high when compared to the general public. Inmates have a lower ability to search for information, comprehend and use the information or carry out computations (Greenberg, et al. 2007).

Strategies to Help Implement Effective Rehabilitation

Despite the benefits of the rehabilitation of inmates, it is important that jail administrators devise good strategies and action points that will ensure the effectiveness of the rehabilitation process. The following action points will be useful in the rehabilitation process:

- There should be the provision of vocational training and educational opportunities for prisoners and offenders with an assessed need.
- Jail administrators can involve friends, families, the community, and volunteers where appropriate, in the rehabilitation process of offenders. Ex-prisoners report that *"Family support was identified as the most important thing that had kept them out of prison"* (Visher & Courtney, 2007).
- During the development and implementation of services and programs, restorative justice approach should be incorporated.

- Ensure that the offender and prisoner programs are of quality standards (Howells et al. 2004).

Characteristics of Effective Rehabilitation That Works

Researchers have over the years made tremendous progress in identifying the characteristics of an effective rehabilitation program that will reduce recidivism; however, the effectiveness of the program varies based on the inmates that participate and the characteristics of the program. The principles explained subsequently have been observed to increase the effectiveness of rehabilitation and reduce recidivism.

Focus on the Criminogenic Needs of Inmates

Criminogenic needs are conditions or problems which individuals require help with that have a history of impacting criminal recidivism. In order to ensure that rehabilitation programs are effective, the criminogenic needs of inmates that have been assessed as having a need in specific areas should be a major target. Some of the major needs that have been identified include:

- Substance abuse
- Low self-control
- Vocational/educational needs
- Antisocial attitudes
- Dysfunctional family environments
- Mental health problems

There should be an assessment of the inmate's needs in order to ascertain if the inmate needs a particular rehabilitation program. The issues that cause the criminality of inmates can be reduced when they are placed in rehabilitation programs that meet their needs, leading the inmate to the less likelihood of reoffending. If they are placed in programs that do not address their needs, it may not only be ineffective, but may lead to a higher chance of recidivism (Ohio Department of Rehabilitation and Correction).

The Risk Principle

Rehabilitation programs should practice the risk principle. "Risk" is the possibility of criminal recidivism based on several historical factors, like the criminal history of the inmate, and also dynamic factors that could change when the inmate is involved in treatments. The intensity of the program relates to how concentrated the rehabilitation program is over the length of time the participant receives rehabilitation. Risk should not be mixed up with the seriousness of a crime. While the highest-risk inmate in a rehabilitation program might have committed theft, the lowest-risk inmate might have committed murder. There is a relationship between the intensity of inmate rehabilitation and risk; high-intensity rehabilitation programs are usually more effective for high-risk offenders.

> *"...we need to recognize that a very large portion of the prison, probation, and parole populations is low risk; these offenders are being punished and even treated beyond their threat to public safety. It's like a hospital that decides to provide intensive care for patients who have a cold— the treatment is not only unnecessary, but expensive."*
>
> *(Austin, 2006)*

The most suitable approach to the rehabilitation of high-risk inmates is the use of the highest level of intensive programs in order to reduce recidivism (Ohio Department of Rehabilitation and Correction).

Proper Implementation of the Program

It is critical that corrections officers execute the rehabilitation program as it was designed and that they do it well in order to get the intended result. When rehabilitation programs lack integrity, it will not have the expected impact on recidivism, and other outcomes will not be available (Van Voorhis & Brown, 1995; MacKenzie, 2006). A good rehabilitation program implementation and integrity are contingent upon the following elements, though not limited to them:

- It should utilize validated risks and needs assessment tools. It is also helpful to identify the inmates' strength.
- Corrections staff should be well-trained to conduct the rehabilitation program, and they need to understand the rationale behind the program. The rehabilitation program should have a manual which the officers should follow.
- A rehabilitation program that makes theoretical sense should be adopted, and it should be based on treatment methods that have proven to be effective.

- The recruitment of prison staff should focus more on staff that have good relationship skills, such as empathy, respect, and enthusiasm.
- Rehabilitation programs should enhance intrinsic motivation. Officers can identify ambivalence about change through motivational interviewing and help to resolve it.
- In order to ensure the quality of the program, it should be evaluated to ensure it conforms to the original design (Ohio Department of Rehabilitation and Correction).

Cognitive-Behavioral and Social Learning Strategies

Inmate rehabilitation should utilize cognitive-behavioral programming and social learning strategies because they are very interactive and help to address the thought process that culminates into criminal behaviors. Cognitive-behavioral programming is based on the assumption that our thinking pattern or how we think controls our feelings and moods and will ultimately control our behaviors.

Such programs help in the identification of the thought process that leads to negative feelings and also maladaptive behaviors. It also helps to replace the wrong thought process with processes that lead to positive feelings and behavior. The effectiveness of cognitive-behavioral programming is backed by results of research that examined findings from many evaluations of different types of treatment which show that the use of cognitive-behavioral rehabilitation is successful in reducing recidivism (Ohio Department of Rehabilitation and Correction).

Continuity of Care

There is a need for relapse prevention and continued care of inmates in the community, especially inmates that are re-entering the community after their incarceration. Several findings from meta-analysis discover that rehabilitation with an aftercare component is actually more effective in reducing the cases of recidivism when compared to rehabilitation without an aftercare component. Participants are able to deal with high-risk situations in the community with the support that is provided in aftercare service.

Correctional Rehabilitation through Education

The educational qualification of inmates tends to be less when compared to the general population. Education is very important in the reduction of criminal activities. Education helps to increase the problem-solving abilities of inmates, their social interaction skills and a sense of self-efficacy. All these are characteristics associated with pro-social behavior. By increasing the skills of inmates, and also their employment opportunities, there will be a reduction in crimes committed for financial gain. It also helps to increase the exposure of offenders to pro-social people and situations which can enhance pro-social behaviors and attitudes (Ohio Department of Rehabilitation and Correction).

Vocational Education

There is a high level of implementation of vocational education in correctional facilities, due to the fact that it deals with the high incidence of academic and employment failure of inmates. Despite the fact that it may be difficult to conclude about the effectiveness of vocational education programs due to the diverse nature of the program, indications from meta-analysis and systemic reviews of vocational education programs show that it helps in the reduction of criminal activities of inmates that participate (Wilson et al., 2000; Wilson et al., 1999; MacKenzie, 2006). It increases the employment rate of offenders, and higher recidivism rates have been associated with lower employment rates.

Life Skills

Life skills programs are quite new when compared to other programs. The reason for the use of life skills programs in correctional facilities is that basic adult educational programs place focus on academic skills and may not be able to address other deficiencies of inmates (Finn, 1998). Although inmates may have serious issues with reading and writing, there are other areas where they may also experience difficulty, like the balancing of a check book, anger control, conducting a job search, setting and meeting life goals and maintaining a healthy interpersonal relationship. Life skills programs are designed to effectively deal with these types of skill deficiencies that may limit the ability of offenders to successfully function in everyday life and integrate into the community.

The implementation of an effective strategy that will help in the rehabilitation of inmates depends on the discipline of the corrections officers and jail administrators. A great strategy will not be effective if it is not properly implemented, and in order to implement a strategy, discipline is required. Proper training of prison staff to enable them to understand the purpose of rehabilitation and effectively supervise prisoners should be pursued. One of the major goals of inmate rehabilitation is to reduce the cases of recidivism and also lower the risk of releasing inmates that may pose a threat to the community.

Keywords: Rehabilitation, Correctional, Prison, Recidivism, Offenders, Treatment, Deterrence, Prisoners, Inmates, Program, Programming, Behavior, Criminal, Inmates.

CHAPTER SEVENTEEN
Effective New Paradigm Shift

Punishment & Counseling Rehabilitation - Historical Perspective

Several research findings have revealed that the punishment and correctional approaches for behavioral change are just as old as most of the correctional facilities around the world. Correctional facilities for a long time have been faced with two challenging missions: protecting the public safety, and also the rehabilitation of offenders (Walters et al. 2007; Kolind, 2010). In the early 1900s, the use of treatment approaches was introduced into the correctional field, and this took place after many years of brutal and dehumanizing prison conditions. Correctional officers were known as guards for a long time; this reflects a security and punitive approach used then by the prisons. Before 1965, the role of guards was clearly defined, and it includes the maintenance of security and internal order (Farkas, 1995).

There is a clear difference between the term "guard" and "correctional officer". While the word guard suggests a custodial identity and also custodial function, a correctional officer shows the deviation from a punishment approach that was initially practiced to a rehabilitative approach in the correctional facilities.

During the mid-1970s, the use of punishment to rehabilitate inmates was practiced, and rehabilitation oriented policies were believed to be responsible for causing trouble in prison. Consequently, the sentencing landscape changed to "get tough" laws which promoted the punishment models. No doubt there have been several changes in the approaches of correctional facilities, but probation and parole officers need to shift from the perception that confrontational approaches are important in behavior change in correctional organizations. It has been argued that the role of correctional officers has been to solidify and not to dissipate in the correctional facilities of the 1990s and beyond (Stohr and Zupan, 1992).

Correctional facilities need to change from a punishment perspective in dealing with inmates to a correctional perspective. This involves a commitment by correctional officers to deter the recurrence of criminal behavior of inmates by applying correctional counseling. They have to change from not only being custodial, but also rehabilitative officers that are ready to help inmates stay permanently away from the prisons. One of the biggest challenges the paradigm change will encounter is handling two key functions: inmate incarceration and rehabilitation (Gatotoh, et al. 2011).

Reasons for Resistance to Paradigm Change

Correctional managers are likely to resist effective paradigm shifts for several reasons, including:

- Correctional managers are internal to the organization and may find it difficult to objectively take a look at issues that involve them.
- The process of change put them at risk, which clearly manifests as uncertainty and fear.
- They are affected by paradigms that have been imbibed for a long time, despite the fact that the paradigm is under serious attack.
- They have developed habits with old methods, and habits are difficult to change.
- Outdated beliefs in correctional systems.

There are several beliefs that are no longer sustainable due the rapid change witnessed in the corrections sector:

- The belief that the corrections industry is an essential industry that will never shut down, which is no longer true.
- High-security facilities will always remain relevant in the system. This is no longer true because of the increasing use of medium and minimum security facilities.
- The belief that correctional facilities are currently run efficiently at its best is no longer true because of the increasing need for cost saving approaches.

The rapid rate at which our society is changing affects virtually every aspect of human endeavor, and correctional facilities are not left out. (Jones & Bartlett Learning)

Change Factors in Correctional Systems

The correctional facilities have witnessed several changes in different areas, and most of these changes have ushered in the need for a new approach to inmate rehabilitation. There are several reasons why there is a need for correctional organizations to quickly adjust to the ever changing trends in our world. Take a look at some of the factors that have led to the change (Jones & Bartlett Learning).

Overcrowding

The crowding rates in prisons have increased drastically, and they continue to increase in some states. There is every tendency that it will continue to increase because of the political and public pressure for harsher and longer sentences. There is a need for better and more effective management of the correctional organization in order to reduce the incidence of the return of inmates.

Budget Concerns

Due to budget pressures, some states have not been able to open newly constructed correctional facilities, because they may not be able to pay their newly recruited staff. This was the case of the state of Arizona many years ago, which postponed the activation of several facilities as a result of staffing problems.

Privatization

What was once the sacred public corrections arena has witnessed the birth of private corrections that run less expensively in comparison to public correctional organizations. They have witnessed several problems, such as escapes, drug use and staff turnover, making their less expensive operation questionable (Camp and Gaes, 2002).

Management of Inmates

As a result of the difficult issues presented by prison and street gangs, it is becoming more difficult to manage inmates. If the correctional organizations lack the resources to effectively manage inmates, then inmates may not be effectively rehabilitated, which increases the likelihood of inmates to return to the facility after their release.

The Management of Workforce

Correctional facilities are also losing personnel either by retirement or by other avenues, and having a lack of competent personnel with the increasing difficulty in handling offenders, a greater challenge. Better working conditions and environments will help to reduce the rate at which employees leave their jobs and also motivate them to put in their best efforts towards a better rehabilitation of inmates.

New Technology

Correctional facilities are witnessing an influx of new technologies, such as perimeter security measures, restrain methodology, drug testing equipment, and remote monitoring equipment. There is a need for staff to understand the effective use and application of these technologies.

Embracing Change

> *"Nothing in progression can rest on its original plan. We might as well think of rocking a grown man in the cradle of an infant."*
>
> *Edmund Burke*

Considering the rapid change in the correctional organization, it is evident that corrections are no longer static fields. The management of correctional facilities need to quickly adapt and adjust to shifting priorities and also prepare for change by considering new workplace strategies. Correctional managers need to start afresh and try to ignore old practices as much as possible. Assistance from outside organizations can be useful in propelling correctional organizations to leave their comfort zones to get creative solutions.

Officers Attitude and Correctional Orientation

A clear understanding of the motivation of correctional officers will help in recruiting better officers and also ensure that inmates are properly rehabilitated. It was observed from a study conducted that there is a positive relationship between the motivation to become a correctional officer on a human service basis and rehabilitation orientation. While officers who want to join correctional organizations on the basis of human service are likely to accept the rehabilitation of inmates (Robinson, et al. 1997), those who joined for the sake of security issues are likely not to support rehabilitation. Other organizational variables that predict the correctional orientation among correctional officers includes rank, role problem, job stress, job satisfaction, seniority, frequency of inmate contact, and facility security level (Gatotoh, et al. 2011).

Correctional Attitudes

Correctional officers need to change their perspectives about correctional attitude. Rather than punishment, counseling should be used in inmate rehabilitation. Based on the statistics of a survey that was conducted by (Gatotoh, et al. 2011), several findings were made concerning the correctional attitude of officers. It was discovered that slightly more than 53.8% of the respondents to the survey believe that the counseling approach is more effective than the punishment approach in rehabilitating inmates, while 38.5% view the punishment approach to be more effective than counseling. This indicates that there are many officers who still believe that punishment is better than counseling in rehabilitating inmates.

There were other findings regarding the attitude of correctional officers. Many officers derive satisfaction from interacting with inmates. This implies that they have a positive attitude towards inmates, and that is a very conducive condition for inmate rehabilitation (Young, 2009). A shift in the approach of correctional officers from punishment to counseling approach will help reduce the incidence of the return of inmates after serving their term, since it is a more effective way of rehabilitating inmates (Gatotoh, et al. 2011).

Correctional Officers' Occupational Attitudes

The occupational attitude of correctional officers relates to their awareness of the responsibility of their profession to the society, their attitude towards their profession and how they would respond to a change in the working conditions. The results of a survey indicate that 42.2% of correctional officers do not consider their job as honorable, while 33.6% believe it is honorable. It is however, remarkable to note that 75% of officers acknowledge that they have a great responsibility to the next generation and the society. A total of 65.4% of the respondents agreed that they will remain in the profession if the working environment is improved.

The implication of the way they perceive their job reflects on the state of their mind; a positive mindset will always help them accept alternative ways of inmate rehabilitation. The occupational attitude of officers is very important in rehabilitating inmates. When they have a positive attitude towards their profession, they will have a better understanding of their duty and the importance of their job (Gatotoh, et al. 2011).

Factors Influencing the Attitudes of Correctional Officers

There are several factors that could affect the attitudes of correctional officers. Some of those factors include the age and rank of the officers (Jackson & Annen, 1996; Jurik & Musheno, 1986; Lariviere & Robinson, 1995; Toch & Klofas, 1982). Older officers were found to show more support for the counseling approach of inmate rehabilitation, rather than a punishment approach.

There is sufficient evidence to suggest that high-ranking officers are generally more comfortable with their jobs than lower-ranking officers (Reising and Lovrich, 1998). Correctional officers at the lower ranks need a better working condition in order to give them a positive attitude towards their work, which will also lead to better performance.

Conclusion

There should be an inclusion of correctional counseling in correctional training. This will equip correctional officers with the proper knowledge, skill, and attitude that is necessary for the rehabilitation of inmates using the behavioral change approach. The working conditions of correctional officers and their correctional facilities, which could be the terms of service, should be improved in order to prevent the demoralization of the workers. The working environments in correctional facilities should foster cooperation among staff and as much as possible reduce the fear of authority. Opportunities for further training should be provided for correctional officers in order to foster better service.

Despite the fact that most correctional officers believe that counseling is effective in inmate rehabilitation, many officers still believe that though counseling helps, they would choose punishment rather than counseling. They need a proper awareness through training to appreciate the importance of counseling in inmate rehabilitation (Gatotoh, et al. 2011).

CHAPTER EIGHTEEN
Effective Ways to Avoid Lawsuits

The United States accommodates the largest number of inmates in the world. In 2013, there were 698 individuals incarcerated per 100,000 population in the United States, and according to the U.S. Bureau of Justice Statistics, in 2013, 2,220,300 adults were imprisoned in federal prisons, state prisons and county jails in the United States. Some of the offenders are litigious and may have filed several lawsuits against administrators, sheriffs' corrections officers, and other workers in correctional facilities.

Considering the fact that many inmates in the correctional institutions know about statutes and regulations and may be more enlightened than many corrections officers, prison staff members need to learn to handle inmates to avoid such lawsuits. Another issue that officers face is the threat of inmates that have filed lawsuits pro-se when they cite past litigation; this makes the execution of their duties difficult for fear of the lawsuits (Osterstuck, 2012).

Litigation is actually the most familiar consequence of poor risk management. It includes claims that are settled by agreement before it is taken to court and formal lawsuits that are filed in court. Those who can initiate a lawsuit include:

- Inmates
- Corrections officers
- Inmates' family members
- Visitors
- Victims of released inmates

- Victims of inmates that escaped
- Volunteers

Conflict Resolution

One of the effective ways that correctional officers can avoid lawsuits is through conflict resolution. When officers are faced with a conflict situation, there are three objectives that should be their focus:

Avoid the Danger

The awareness of a possible threat is a crucial aspect of avoiding the danger. The earlier corrections officers perceive a possible threat from inmates, the more time they have to assess the situation and take a better course of action. Officers also need to be aware of their location or surroundings and other factors in making a decision on how to deal with an issue. The factors and locations could be alarm bells, exits, the nearness of colleagues and other inmates.

Defuse the Situation

In a bid to manage violence from escalating, officers need to utilize communication and de-escalation skills as much as possible. The best defensive weapons for correction officers are verbal and non-verbal communication skills. Most officers that employ the use of effective communication skills will be able to defuse a potential conflict, although in some cases, the most reasonable approaches may not stop the officer from the use of force. When an officer is defusing a situation, threats should not be used. Once an ultimatum or threat is given, all negotiations will cease, and this puts the officers in a potential win-or-lose situation. In order to effectively defuse the violence, the actions of officers need to include the following:

- Officers need to speak slowly, clearly and gently.
- There is a need for a confident appearance; officers need to create the impression that they are capable of handling the situation.
- Corrections officers should not argue.
- Always display calmness and take note of body language.
- Officers should listen and let the inmates know that they are listening.
- Give them some space and provide a sense of safety for the inmates.

- Ask questions.
- The voice of the officer should be low; this might also lower the voices of the inmates.

Control the Situation

Officers need to adopt a positive, assertive and confident approach to reducing the possibility of being a victim of unwanted attention. Corrections officers should avoid being trapped in a corner, and they should encourage reasoning when dealing with inmates.

Although the use of conflict resolution strategies can resolve some issues, there are times when the use of force by corrections officers is inevitable. In such situations, the use of control and restraint techniques will definitely be a better option, and when the situation needs other means of protection, officers can adopt the use of batons and other personal safety measures (PSO 1600, 2015).

Reasons Why Inmates File Lawsuits

There are several reasons why inmates file lawsuits against officers and institutions, like discrimination and medical care issues. According to a national survey conducted in 2003 by Margo Schlanger, entitled "Inmate Litigation", the list of the most prevalent litigation issues for jails include:

Medical Care Issues

Inmates usually have medical and mental health needs, and many of these health issues are related to addictions. Officers should keep a record of the requests made by inmates for medical care and also notify the medical department of any claims made. In order to limit the number of lawsuits on medical grounds, officers need to adopt a strong sick call practice and medical rounds in cell units (Horgan, 2011).

Correctional facilities should provide protocol and services that will identify inmates' health care needs, provide access to the needed health care and manage the delivery of health care services. Some health care issues that could lead to lawsuits include:

- Inadequate training of corrections staff that perform health assessment and screening during the intake process.
- Inadequate assessment and screening of procedures and instruments.

- Inadequate resources that are meant to help manage alcohol, drug withdrawal and detoxification.
- Not being able to identify the need for suicide prevention and intervention services.
- Lack of access to qualified medical health care staff that will oversee and deliver quality health care services.
- Inadequate emergency services in the correctional facility.
- Gaps in the availability of and access to a continuum of health care services, which includes dental, medical and mental health.
- Insufficient protocols for the control of communicable and infectious diseases.

Control Strategies to Health Issues

In order to reduce the number of lawsuits as a result of poor health care, correctional facilities should take note of the following strategies:

- Maintain adequate food service operations by employing qualified food service staff, implementing a comprehensive food services sanitation plan and provision of an adequate nutritional diet. Others are provision of therapeutic diets where needed, provision of training in food preparation and sanitation practices in jail facilities and full compliance with the applicable food service and sanitation codes.
- Make provisions for basic health care needs of the inmates by developing and implementing health service plans that will provide for continuity of care from the admission of the inmate to the discharge, which includes referral to community providers outside the jail if needed.
- Qualified health care staff should be employed.
- A program to help control communicable diseases and infections should be established.
- The facilities, supplies, and resources that inmates need in order to maintain acceptable levels of personal hygiene should be provided.
- There should be provision for health care services of offenders that have special needs, which could be those that are chronically ill, mentally or physically disabled, geriatric or developmentally

disabled and those who have serious mental illness (Martin et al. 2008).

Sanitation and Living Conditions

Several lawsuits are as the result of the conditions of inmates' confinement, particularly in older and overcrowded correctional facilities. Officers should deal with problems that inmates complain about no matter how little they may be; this will give the inmates a sense of care. Their living conditions should be as humane as possible, with fast and effective follow up on any issue that will make their confinement safer (Horgan, 2011).

Classification Issues

A good classification plan is very important to correctional facilities. There is a need for fairness in dealing with inmate classification. Inmates deserve the chance to earn privileges like spending more time out of their cells, a lower security level, and more visits as a result of good behavior. Inmates that are involved in an altercation may perceive what they feel is faulty classification decision and therefore take legal action. Corrections officers who get a request for a change in classification status by inmates need to forward them promptly to classification (Horgan, 2011).

Food and Special Diet Requests

Inmates will always demand religious or medical diets, and one of the effective ways of ensuring that legitimate requests for religious diets are granted is by allowing a chaplain to review such requests. This will ensure that the possibility of litigation is greatly reduced. Also, the medical staff needs to review all requests for medical diets, and a nutritionist can review the menu in order to ensure that the nutritional and caloric guidelines are satisfied.

The factors that could lead to poor food service in corrections facilities include:

- Improper practices in the food preparation
- Poor level of sanitation in food service facilities
- Unqualified food service staff
- Poor storage and cooking of food
- The use of food that was contaminated before getting to the facility
- Poor screening of food suppliers

- Inadequate menu and diet plan, which also includes the provision for special needs
- Noncompliance with health, food service and safety codes
- Inadequate training of food service staff in the preparation of food and sanitation practices

Other reasons why inmates file lawsuits against corrections officers include:

- Use of force
- Personal injury
- Crowding
- Damage to property
- Law library services
- Inmate-on-inmate violence
- Suicide prevention
- Disciplinary procedures

The Effectiveness of the Training Academy

The first and basic source of learning to handle lawsuits as a corrections officer is the training academy. Prison staff members are taught the basics of how to prevent lawsuits, and also they are taught about new legal practices that may likely have an impact on corrections officers. The training places focus on the following areas:

- A review of policies and procedures
- The study of law
- How to manage violent and mentally ill inmates
- The training teaches about role-playing exercises
- Provides information about techniques for dealing with inmates

Although, the jail staff provide the direction for the correctional facility and are responsible for the general security and control of the facility, they have an individual responsibility to know about the latest correctional legal issues. Officers can achieve this by attending conferences, training, reviewing the available training materials through the warden's office, joining professional organizations and several other avenues.

Prisoner Litigation Reform Act (PLRA)

As a result of the increased number of prisoner litigation, federal regulations have made it more difficult for offenders to file frivolous suits against officers. The prisoner litigation reform act has three major components:

- Offenders are expected to have exhausted all possible administrative remedies before they can file a case in the federal court
- Inmates filing petitions in forma pauperis need to pay the applicable fees and also the court cost from their existing funds that may be available through correctional trust fund accounts
- Offenders are prohibited from filing in forma pauperis if previous petitions filed have been dismissed as malicious or frivolous (Campbell, 2009)

The denial of the constitutional rights of an inmate, which includes the right to freedom to access the court, freedom of religion, freedom of recreation and freedom to speak, could lead to a lawsuit in federal court. Most inmates are well-versed in the law, which means that officers should have a great understanding of the law and also act professionally when carrying out their duties.

Inmates Perception of Justice and Fairness

The inmates' perception of justice and fairness in the policies and procedures of correctional facilities is a major reason for lawsuits. The inmates' rights and responsibilities have been established by the legal system; therefore, correctional institutions must comply with legal mandates, and officers need to deal with offenders in an impartial and fair manner. There is an increase in the number of litigations when correctional facilities lack fundamental fairness, and also when an appropriate balance has not been reached on how to maintain security, safety, and order and their obligation to the rights of the offenders. Some of the contributing factors to inmates' perceived injustice and lack of fairness include:

- Extremely restrictive policies that limit the offender's communication and access to the courts
- The failure of the institution to maintain a viable grievance process
- The inability of the prison authorities to afford appropriate levels of due process in disciplinary issues
- Jail conditions that subject inmates to personal abuse, such as harassment, personal injury, corporal punishment and loss of property

- When there is perceived discrimination in administrative decisions on the basis of religion, race, sexual orientation, disability, gender and national origin
- Lack of the opportunities for offenders to make restitution or to satisfy court obligations
- The absence of parity between female and male inmates in the access to programs and services (Martin, et al. 2008)

Litigation Control Strategies

In order to reduce the number of lawsuits filed by inmates or others against corrections officers and jail administrators, the following strategies will be useful:

- Develop and strictly adhere to a written process for dealing with rule violations and administering discipline. Provide information regarding the process during inmate orientation, and it should be included in the inmate's handbook.
- A legitimate grievance process should be established. It should be transparent enough to prevent inmates from perceiving it as a pretense.
- Corrections officers should be well trained to treat offenders fairly and also in a non-discriminatory manner. Officers need to adhere to the jail's justice-related procedures and policies.
- Administrators should assess and address equity and parity issues that relate to inmates' access to programs and services. Inmates should be provided with resources that they need to satisfy other court requirements or make restitution (Martin, et al. 2008).

Record keeping is essential in all cases where offenders are subdued by jail staff, because the documentation of the events and actions will save officers from making wrong statements or testimony about the incident. If officers wish to deny inmates their constitutional rights, there should be proper documentation to indicate that the inmate has violated his/her rights by doing something not allowed by the correctional facility intentionally. A good example will be inmates that fight during recreation, which will be the justification to place the inmate in administrative segregation from other prisoners in order to ensure the safety of the facility.

Keywords: Litigation, Lawsuit, Jail, Prison, Use of force, Control, Defuse, Conflict Resolution, Justice, Fairness, Procedure, Policies, Inmate.

CHAPTER NINETEEN
Effective Ways to Manage a Correctional Facility

Managers and directors of correctional facilities did not recognize their job as managers of large and complex organizations until recently. This perception has gradually changed at the end of the twentieth century. A businessman and author of a report on the management of the Prison Service of England and Wales wrote that:

> *The Prison Service is the most complex organization I have encountered, and its problems, some of the most intractable*
>
> *(Lygo, 1991).*

In managing correctional facilities, prison administrators need to first identify the challenges they face as leaders; this includes both their daily challenges and also broader challenges they need to deal with in order to bring their correctional facility into compliance with international human rights standards and norms. One of the best methods that prison managers can adopt in order to move the institution forward is to organize a brainstorming session where all the participants are invited to verbalize their opinions about the challenges they face, and both negative and positive experiences should be allowed.

Although, every worker should be given the opportunity to contribute, care should be taken to ensure that the session does not turn into an opportunity for individuals to talk about every single frustration they have in their work lives. It should be a platform where participants will have the opportunity to partake in planning, problem solving and suggestions on creative solutions to issues facing the institution.

Leaders need to strike a balance between the safety and security of offenders so as to prevent them from causing harm to themselves and other inmates and the rehabilitation of inmates so that they will be able to integrate back into the society and live a very productive lives. The role of the correctional institutions is very crucial in maintaining order in the society and also securing the lives of inmates. There is a need for leaders to equip themselves with the right knowledge needed to fulfill this task.

Effective Management of Change

A systems approach to managing change involves the understanding and managing of interrelated processes as a system. This will enhance the effectiveness of organization and the efficiency in the achievement of its objectives. The system approach involves:

- A systematic definition of the initiatives or the necessary activities needed to obtain the desired change
- Establishing clear responsibility and also delegating authority to the individuals charged with these responsibilities
- Establishing accountability for managing key initiatives or activities
- Analyzing and understanding the potential and also the real impact of key activities and initiatives
- Identification of the interconnectedness of major activities/initiatives within and between the functions of the organization
- Focusing on key factors like methods, resources, tools and materials that will ensure the success of major activities and initiatives
- Effectively monitor the impact of the key activities and initiatives, taking note of the feedback on the change produced, and also readjusting the activities/initiatives when necessary

Effective Prison Management

The effective and efficient management of correctional facilities is based on several key functions and activities, and many leaders need to focus on these areas in order to foster better prison management (UNODC, 2010).

Human Resource Management

There is no doubt that the most important aspect of prison management is the efficient management of the staff. Human resource management has to do with the effective use of individuals in an organization to increase performance, which will lead to the attainment of organizational objectives. In order to achieve this goal, leaders need to hire the best people to handle the job and also develop and empower them within the positions they occupy.

Another important point to enhance the performance of the staff is by improving internal communication among the correction officers and between the managers and the staff. This will increase the morale of the employee, encourage individual responsibility and initiative, support a collaborative approach and reduce the level of grievances in the organization.

Stores and Procurement Management

Correctional institutions need to have a system that will ensure that there is value for money spent and also that the procurement of goods is in a timely and efficient manner in order to enhance the effective operation of the facility. While some procurements may be done centrally by government agencies, other procurements can be carried out by the prison service as a whole or by the individual correctional facility. The process of procurement should be guided by clear guidelines and policies and should be meticulously documented.

Considering the fact that the procurement management function is prone to corrupt practices, there is a need for close and efficient monitoring of this function by senior managers. Another crucial aspect of resource management is store management, and it has to operate under fairly detailed guidelines and policies. Regular inventory of equipment and stores needs to be conducted and maintained, and there should be proper documentation of the use of all materials, food stores, supplies, and others in order to allow for regular inspection and effective planning for the purchasing, production, distribution and utilization of stores and equipment (UNODC, 2010).

Correctional Facility Management

The facility's management refers to the services that are required to ensure the development and maintenance of the correctional facility. It determines the tasks that need to be done and who should do them. Some of the services that need to be done in a correctional facility include:

- Health care
- Construction
- Laundry
- Maintenance
- Food preparation

In some organizations, in order to effectively achieve organizational goals, there is a balance between internal and outsourced management of tasks; however, every process that is involved in the accomplishment of the objectives of the organization needs to be transparent and also determined by cost efficiency. It is important to be conscious of the security of the facility and also the importance of employing inmates where possible.

Financial Resource Management in Prisons

There is a need for organizations to implement financial management processes. It will ensure financial sustainability, integrity, and accountability. The financial process must be based on sound accounting practices and budgeting. Jail administrators need to adopt and consistently apply accepted standards of accounting practices in order to give room for independent audits and reviews, which will support financial accountability to external and internal stakeholders. The accounting, budgeting and reporting practices of correctional facilities need to be well-aligned with the best government practices obtained in other sectors. There should also be an implementation of a system of checks and balances within the prison's financial resource management system in order to verify accountability for all spending and also deter corruption (UNODC, 2010).

Prisons Security Management

Managers of correctional facilities need to also take the security and safety of the facility seriously so as to prevent inmates from escaping and also to prevent attackers from gaining access to the facility. The correctional facilities should have a set level of security, the level of security of the correctional facility depends on the nature of the prison and also the necessity of security from the people outside the organization or the threat that is posed by the potential escape of inmates. The security of the facility should be developed in line with a developed security policy for the facility which outlines the specific functions and objectives.

Meeting the Basic Needs of Inmates

Jail administrators need to understand the international standards and norms relating to the basic needs of inmates. By knowing about the standards, administrators will be able to know if the standards are complied with within the correctional facility, and if not, they should know the reasons why and seek practical ways to ensure that the basic needs of inmates are effectively met. The basic needs of inmates include:

- **Accommodation** - All the accommodation that is provided for the inmates, which include sleeping accommodation, shall meet all health requirements, and climatic conditions should be considered, especially the cubic air content of air, lighting, ventilation, and minimum floor space and heating.
- **Adequate Clothing and Bedding** - If the inmates are not permitted to wear their clothes, they should be given clothing that is suitable for the climate and sufficient to maintain good health. The clothes should in no way be humiliating or degrading.
- **Good Food** - Inmates should have access to foods which have nutritional values that are adequate for health and strength. Foods should be of wholesome quality, well prepared and served.
- **Exercise and Sports** - Inmates are entitled daily to at least one hour of suitable exercise in the open air, provided the weather is favorable for the exercise.
- **Medical Services** - Prison facilities should have the services of at least one qualified medical officer, and the medical officer should have a good knowledge of psychiatry. The health issues of inmates should be taken care of, and prisoners that require special treatment should be transferred to specialized institutions or to civil hospitals (UNODC, 2010).

The Management of Disciplinary Process

One of the objectives of prisons is to carry out the penalties that have been imposed by the courts and not to impose more punishment. There is a need for a high level of structure and order in prisons, especially within medium and maximum security institutions. The discipline that is needed in a correctional facility should be balanced with a great sense of safety and mutual respect. In a well-managed system, there should not be a high level of fear and a strong feeling of insecurity among inmates and staff.

According to the international standards and norms, the disciplinary process must be well-defined and explained in existing prisons' policies and guidelines. There should be a clear definition of the role of managers in the process, and there should be a proper documentation of the action and process that led to every disciplinary action that is taken. The training of staff should address in detail, the disciplinary policies and processes in place within the correctional facility and the role of the corrections staff within the process. There should be checks and balances that will help to reduce the level of abuse of the process in order to make the disciplinary process effective (UNODC, 2010).

Management of Information

Information management can increase knowledge and efficiency in the management of prisons when there is an effective system of collection of data, storage, usage and disposal of data. Corrections officers should have access to data based on their job description, while other data should be protected. Sensitive information regarding correction officers and offenders should be kept confidential and also released to people strictly on a "need to know" basis, while prison managers should have access to good data regarding the population of the facility, the facilities, staff and every resource in the correctional facility. The availability of such information will help jail administrators to plan effectively for the future operations and other aspects of prison management (UNODC, 2010).

Management of Prison Population

The core function of a prison is to accommodate individuals awaiting trial, those already on trial, detainees awaiting sentence and those already fulfilling their sentence. These categories of detainees should be kept separately, according to international standards.

How to Take Charge of an Organization Fast

Taking over the control of an organization has several challenges, and one of the challenges include the strategies that an individual has in order to maintain the current success of the organization and also take the organization to the next level of success. The following tips will help every jail administrator in taking over a new facility:

- **Commence the Transition before the Job** - By making use of the interview process, leaders can obtain valuable information regarding the organization as early as possible. There is the need to ask vital questions, such as:
  - What are the major challenges facing the correctional facility?
  - How are decisions made?
  - Which functions need to be overhauled, and which ones are strong?
- Having answers to these questions will help leaders with the necessary information to make a positive change in the institution. Take your cue from Steve Bennett, who took over the CEO spot at Intuit Corp.

"The interview process is where you start... that's where you ask all of the questions about what it takes to be successful."

- **Listen Effectively** - Leaders need to listen effectively and ask questions, relate with employees and talk to all levels of employees; that way, a clear picture of what is happening within the organization will be disclosed.
- **Select Your Team** - While listening and asking questions, leaders should be able to identify key players that possess the skills needed to achieve set goals, and most likely the people with good answers are enlightened to be part of the team.
- **Acknowledge What You Do Not Know** - There are things that leaders do not know; however, leaders should identify individuals who are experts and leverage on their expertise in solving problems.
- **Listen to People who disagree** - It is important to listen to individuals who challenge your assumptions. You will be able to get more information needed to make a balanced decision.
- **Clean the House if you have to** - Based on the situation, leaders also need to know that despite their vision and goals, there are employees that are too jaded to follow. Such employees should be handled properly.
- **Appreciate Your Predecessor** - Leaders should not trash their predecessor. Despite the fact that the previous administration might have

lost the big picture, they had a different challenge they were working on. Just implement the strategies that will fix the challenges.

- **Make Mistakes, But Fix Them Fast** - There will be mistakes with new positions, and probably new organizations. Taking over a new position or new correctional facility can cause prison managers to make a mistake, but there is a need to fix them faster than they were made (Leadership, 2002).

There are several challenges that a leader encounters in managing a correctional facility, and this is because it houses offenders with diverse health issues, and individuals with criminal tendencies. The different categories of offenders accommodated by correctional facilities include offenders that have been sentenced, individuals awaiting trial after being accused of committing an offense and those who have been convicted of an offense and are awaiting their sentence. Obviously, the job of a prison leader is a very challenging one, and it requires the total commitment of a dedicated, strong and persevering individual to achieve the purpose of the prison.

Summary

Managers of correctional facilities are faced with several challenges when they take over a new facility. They also face emotional challenges, which could be a combination of good and bad emotions. Jail administrators could face the challenges of no routine or unfamiliar routine, which may lead to increased stress and low performance. They are saddled with the responsibility of not only maintaining the current standard of the facility, but also improving on the standard of the facility by coming up with a program or strategy.

Whether managers are taking over the leadership of a new facility or an existing facility, it is important to devote time and energy to establishing how teams will work. The first week is quite critical, because people form opinions quickly, and most of these opinions tend to be sticky. To strategize on how the team will work, problems may occur if care is not taken. Managers should understand and know members of the team, and leaders should focus on fostering camaraderie rather than focusing mainly on the outcome of tasks.

While interacting with the staff of correctional facilities, managers should learn to showcase their values and the reasons behind every decision that they make, their priorities and the method of evaluation of the performance of correctional staff, individually and collectively as a team. While there are goals already for the team, it is also important to clarify the goals that have been set to enable the officers to understand what is expected of them. Managers should also keep their door open and tend to over-communicate rather than not communicate well within the early days of working in a new facility (O'Hara, 2014).

The 30-60-90 Day Strategy

The first step towards an effective work life in a new organization is to develop an effective plan. A plan will provide a blueprint of the management goals and also help to keep track of the progress made. One effective strategy that will help managers of correctional institutions is the 30/60/90 day plan, which spans through the first 30 days, 60 days and 90 days on the job.

30-Days

The first thirty days is also the learning stage for correctional officers and jail administrators. It is important that correctional officers and managers first understand and learn about the new facility. The following points should be considered:

- There is a need to understand the mission and vision statement of the agency, and also the core values of the agency.
- It is important that the overall culture of the facility should also be investigated.
- Managers of correctional agencies also need to familiarize themselves with the staff of the facility.
- There should be an assessment of the structures and facilities in the agency so as to know where changes are needed.

60-Days

After assessing the agency and the core values of the organization, managers have the needed information to enable them to know where changes are needed. The following tips can help in progressing to the next level:

- Jail administrators should progressively start to build their own personal brand and their strategies.
- It is important to brainstorm on personal strategies that will help

in resolving identified issues and also in consolidating on present successes of the agency.

- Managers of correctional institutions should at this stage listen more than they talk.
- Effective communication is also very important. They should be ready to communicate their vision and goals in taking the facility forward.

90-Days

After spending 60 days in the new organization, managers now have a better understanding of how things work and would have developed more confidence. The following points will help in proper management of the facility:

- Be attentive and aware of new projects, and also be ready to provide possible solutions.
- Managers should have a good knowledge of the staff of the facility.
- Analyze the level of growth in the facility.
- Manage every mistake that may have occurred due to inadequate information.
- Identify growth and progress made, which will serve as motivation.

Although jail administrators need to understand the current state of the facility which will involve the identification of problems that the correctional institution faces, it is important that they assign a level of importance to each of the issues and also assess the type of changes needed to solve the problems. Leaders should also envision and lay out their desired future of the facility, and this will include picturing how the ideal facility should be after the strategies and change have been implemented, and also communicating this picture to every stakeholder.

Huhman, H.R. 2012. Follow The '30-60-90' Plan When Starting A New Job: Glassdoor.

Keywords: Managers, Correctional Facility, Management, Directors, Leaders, Prison, Offenders, Inmates, Administrators, Staff, Correction officers.

Conclusion

"The pessimist complains about the wind. The optimist expects it to change. The leader adjusts the sails."

John Maxwell

Effective leadership is a critical factor that determines the success of every organization, and this includes correctional facilities. Most problems and challenges that correctional institutions face can be resolved with good leadership, and considering the increasing challenges facing correctional institutions, officers need to be well-trained and mentored to enable them to deal with new challenges as well as achieve the primary goal of the agency, which is to ensure the safety of staff, inmates and society.

One of the biggest challenges that correctional facilities face presently is the issue of inmates with mental illness. The number of inmates with mental illness has been on the increase, and therefore there is a need to carry out a proper assessment of the mental health of inmates at the intake level before they are allowed into the facility. By assessing their state of health, correctional officers will be able to know inmates that require some form of treatment and attention. The information regarding the mental health of inmates will be useful when conducting inmate classification and reclassification.

Although the isolation of inmates is a strategy used in dealing with violent inmates and inmates with special cases, it should be used with care. Because of the health issues associated with the solitary confinement of inmates, it should only be used when other alternatives are not suitable for dealing with the inmate. Inmates in solitary confinement should not be confined for a long time. The placement of inmates in solitary confinement must be reviewed constantly at short intervals, and mentally ill inmates must not be isolated; this is to avoid the aggravation of their mental health. Isolated inmates should be given access to vocational and educational programs and also allowed to indulge in activities that bring them in contact with other inmates where possible.

There are guidelines that control the use of force in correctional facilities. It should only be used as a last resort, and such use of force should be recorded, including the conversation of all those present when force was used. The video will help in several ways: it will help in evaluating the actions of the officers involved in order to correct possible mistakes, and also it will help in case there is a lawsuit as a result of the incident. Officers should know that the use of force can only be justified by several conditions: when it is necessary, when it is proportionate to the level of seriousness of the incidence, when it is reasonable in the circumstances and when no more force than required is used.

Communication is a major factor in the de-escalation of crises in correctional facilities. Effective communication involves empathic listening. Officers should give inmates their undivided attention when trying to de-escalate a crises situation, acknowledge their feelings and be non-judgmental. In de-escalation of crises, the officers need to also clarify messages to prevent misinterpretation of instructions or statements made. When officers learn how to effectively de-escalate crises, the need for the use of force will be greatly reduced.

In situations of emergencies such as natural disasters and other crises that will require the evacuation of the facility, a good emergency preparedness plan will enhance the comprehensive evacuation of the facility. Jail administrators should ensure that they have good emergency preparedness measures to prevent the escape of inmates and also reduce the level of casualties that may arise as a result of such emergencies. There is no substitute for realistic full evacuation drills. Officers must prove that they are capable of evacuating all inmates from the building, and there must be a regular practice of the evacuation plan. In the event of a large-scale evacuation of offenders, it is very important that departments should authorize an emergency inmate processing and receiving the policy; this will enable the receiving institution to have flexibility in the intake procedures.

One of the benefits of the audit of correctional facilities is to reduce the incidence of corruption and also ensure the effectiveness of the services of correctional institutions. It fosters accountability and strict adherence to policies and procedures. It also provides the agencies with the true picture of the facility, revealing areas of weaknesses and strength which will enable the administrators to make the necessary adjustments. One of the effective ways to have a hitch-free audit of the facility is for correctional institutions to carry out a self-audit before the actual audit; this will help make the audit a fast and easy one.

Correctional officers need to constantly improve their knowledge base. The more enlightened officers are, the more equipped they will be in dealing with several issues they encounter. New and effective techniques are being developed constantly, and through seminars and constant training, officers can learn such techniques. The Department of Justice Division of NIC offers excellent training on key elements in jail administration, jail resource management and also building a productive relationship between jail officials and their funding authority.

They also sponsor a peer-training network for large jail administrators, which includes an online discussion forum. There are numerous organizations that can offer professional development and personal development resources for officers and administrators, including the American Jail Association (AJA) and American Correctional Association (ACA). The training and development of administrators and officers is a major step in ensuring that correctional facilities are effective in meeting their goals.

References

Abner, C.E., Clark, J., and Browning J. 2009. *Preventing And Responding to Corrections-Based Sexual Abuse*: A Guide For Community Corrections Professionals

Adams, K., and Ferrandino, J. (2008). *Managing Mentally Ill Inmates in Prisons*: *Criminal Justice and Behavior*, Vol. 35 No. 8, 913-927

Adult Facility Security Audits*: South Dakota Department of Corrections Policy Distribution*. Public, (2015).

American Correctional Association (ACA): *Agency Manual of Accreditation Policy and Procedure*. (2014).

American Psychiatric Association. (2004). *Mental illness and the criminal justice system*: *Redirecting resources toward treatment, not containment.* Arlington, VA: Author.

Andrews, D. A., and Bonta, J. (2003). *The Psychology of Criminal Conduct* (3rd ed.). Cincinnati, OH: Anderson.

Andrews, D. A., and Bonta, J. (2003). *The Psychology of Criminal Conduct*. Cincinnati, OH: Anderson.

Appelbaum, K.A., Hickey, J.M., and Packer, P. (2001). *The role of correctional officers in multi-disciplinary mental health care in prisons.* Psychiatric Services, 52, 1343-1347.

Arthur, D. (2001). *The Employee Recruitment and Retention Handbook.* New York: American Management Association.

Austin, J. (2006). "*How Much Risk Can We Take? The Misuse of Risk Assessment in Corrections.*" Federal Probation, 70(2): 58-63.

Austin, J. (2003). *Findings in Prison Classification and Risk Assessment.* Washington, DC: National Institute of Corrections.

Austin, J. (1998). *Objective Jail Classification Systems: A Guide for Jail Administrators,* National Institute of Corrections.

Ax, R.K., Fagan, T.J., Magaletta, P.R., Morgan, R.D., Nussbaum, D., and White, T.W. (2007). *Innovations in correctional assessment and treatment. Criminal Justice and Behavior,* 34, 893-905.

Axelrod, Robert. (1984). *The Evolution of Cooperation.* New York: Basic.

Beck, A.J., Harrison, P.M., and Adams, D.B. (2007). *Sexual Victimization in State and Federal Prisons Reported by Inmates,* 2006. Bureau of Justice Statistics Special Report. Washington, DC: U.S. Department of Justice, Office of Justice Programs, Bureau of Justice Statistics.

Beck, A.J., and Maruschak, L.M. (2001). *Mental health treatment in state prisons,* 2000. Bureau of Justice Statistics special report. Washington, DC: Government Printing Office.

Beijersbergen, K.A. (2013). *Procedural Justice in Prison: The Importance of Staff Characteristics.* Netherlands Institute for the Study of Crime and Law Enforcement (NSCR), Amsterdam, The Netherlands.

Bennis, W., and Burt, N. (1985). *Leaders: The Strategies for Taking Charge.* New York: Harper Perennial.

Bies, R. J., and Moag, J. (1986). *Interactional justice: Communication criteria of fairness.* In R. J. Lewicki, B. H. Sheppard, and M. Bazerman (Eds.), Research on negotiation in organizations (Vol. 1, pp. 43–55). Greenwich, CT: JAI Press.

Billsberry, J. (2007). *Experiencing recruitment and selection.* Hoboken, NJ: Wiley & Sons.

Blake, R.R., and J.S. Mouton. (1964). *The managerial grid.* Houston: Gulf Publishing.

Blanding, M. (2008). *Ten steps corrections directors can take to strengthen performance.* Washington, D.C.: Pew Center on the States.

Bocean, C. (2009). *Staff performance management,* Bucharest: Economic Tribune.

Boswell, W.R., and Boudreau, J.W. (2000). *Employee satisfaction with performance appraisals and appraisers:* The role of perceived appraisal use, Human Resource Development Quarterly, vol.11, pp.283–299.

Bosworth, M., and Carrabine, E. (2001). *'Reassessing resistance: race, gender, and sexuality in prison'*, Punishment and Society, 3: 501-515.

Boushey, H., and Sarah, J.G. (2012). *There Are Significant Business Costs to Replacing Employees*: Center for American Progress

Boyer, D. K. (2004). *"The race to address the challenges of the 21st Century workforce."* Corrections Today 66(5): 8, 30.

Breaugh, J. A., Macan, T.H., and Grambow, D. M. (2008). *Employee recruitment: Current knowledge and directions for future research.* In G. P. Hodgkinson & J. K. Ford (Eds.), International Review of Industrial and Organizational Psychology, vol. 23. (pp. 45–82)New York: John Wiley & Sons.

Breaugh, J. A., and Starke, M. (2000). *Research on employee recruitment: So many studies, so many remaining questions.* Journal of Management, 26, 405–434.

Brevis, T., Vrba, M. J., Smit, P.J., and Cronje, G.J. (2007). *Management Principles: A Contemporary Edition for Africa.* 4th Edition. Cape Town: Juta and Co. Ltd.

Buckingham, M. (2005). *What great managers do.* Harvard Business Review, 83(3):70-79.

Buss, A.H., and Buss, E.H. (1969). *Schizophrenia: Seven Approaches.* Transaction Publishers, New Brunswick, NJ.

Byrne, J., Taxman, F., Hummer, D. (2005) *"Examining the Impact of Institutional Culture (and culture change) on Prison Violence and Disorder*: A Review of the Evidence on Both Causes and Solutions," paper presented at the 14th World of Congress of Criminology, Philadelphia, PA. August 11, 2005

Byrne, J.M., and Roberts, A.R. (2007). *New directions in offender typology design, development, and implementation*: Can we balance risk, treatment, and control? Aggression and Violent Behavior, 12, 483-492.

California Department of Corrections and Rehabilitation (CDCR): Use of Force. Title 15, California Code of Regulations, Division 4, Chapter 3, Subchapter 3, Article 2http://www.cdcr.ca.gov/regulations/juvenile_justice/docs/useofforce.pdf

Camp, G.M., and Camp, C.G. (1985). *Prison gangs*: Their extent, nature, and impact on prisons. Washington, DC: U.S. Government Printing Office.

Camp, S. D., and Gaes, G. G. (2002). *Growth and Quality of U.S. Private Prisons*: Evidence from a National Survey. Criminology & Public Policy, 1(3), 427–450

Campbell, D.J., Campbell, K.M., and Chia, H. (1998). *Merit pay, performance appraisal, and individual motivation*: An analysis and alternative, Human Resource Management Journal, vol.37, pp.131–146.

Campbell, N. M. (2005). *Correctional Leadership Competencies for the 21st Century*: Executives and Senior-Level Leaders. Washington, DC: U.S. Department of Justice, National Institute of Corrections, NIC Accession Number 020474

Campbell, N.M. (2006). *Correctional Leadership Competencies for the 21st Century*: Manager and Supervisor Level. Washington, DC: U.S. Department of Justice, National Institute of Corrections, NIC Accession Number 020475

Campbell, T. (2014). *Managing Prison Gangs/Security Threat Groups*: Corrections.com. http://www.corrections.com/news/article/35652-managing-prison-gangs-security-threat-groups

Campbell, T. (2009). *Prison Litigation and What It Means To You as a Corrections Professional.* http://www.corrections.com/news/article/22872-prison-litigation-and-what-it-means-to-you-as-a-corrections-professional

Ceresnie, A. (2009). *The Cost of Long-Term Isolation*: A Need for Accountability and Policy Safeguards in Supermax Prisons Across the United States. Adler School of Professional Psychology.

Chen, H.M., and Kuo, T.S. (2004). *Performance appraisal across organizational lifecycles*, Human Resource Management Journal, vol.23, pp.227–23

Chişu, V.A. (2002). *Manual specialist in human resources*: Irecson, Bucharest.

Clear, T. (1999). *Leading from and leading toward*: Three suggestions. Correctional Management Quarterly, 3 (1): 16.

Clem, C., Krauth, B., and Wenger, P. (2000). *Recruitment, Hiring, and Retention*: Current Practice in U.S. Jails. LIS, Inc.,

Clements, C.B., Althouse, R., Ax, R.K., Magaletta, P.R., Fagan, T.J., and Wormith, J.S. (2007). *Systemic issues and correctional outcomes*: Expanding the scope of correctional psychology. Criminal Justice and Behavior, (34)7, 919-932. DOI: 10.1177/0093854807301561.

Cohen, F. (2008). *Penal isolation: Beyond the seriously mentally ill.* Criminal Justice and Behavior, 35(8), 1017-1047. DOI: 10.1177/0093854808317569.

Cohen-Charash, Y., and Spector, P. E. (2001). *The role of justice in organizations: A meta-analysis.* Organizational Behavior and Human Decision Processes, 86, 278–321.

Colquitt, J. A., Conlon, D. E., Wesson, M. J., Porter, C. O., & Ng, K. Y. (2001). *Justice at the millennium: A meta-analytic review of 25 years of organizational justice research.* Journal of Applied Psychology, 86, 425–445.

Covey, S.R. (2004). *The 7 habits of highly effective people*: restoring the character ethic. New York: Free Press.

Crisis Prevention Institute (CPI). (2003). *De-escalation Tips.* http://www.crisisprevention.com/Resources/Knowledge-Base/De-escalation-Tips

Cropanzano, R., Goldman, B., and Benson, L. (2005). *Organizational justice.* In J. Barling, E. Kelloway, & M. Frone (Eds.), Handbook of work stress (pp. 63–87). Thousand Oaks, CA: Sage.

Decker, S.H., Bynum, T.S., and Weisel, D.L. (1998). *Gangs as organized crime groups*: A tale of two cities. Justice Quarterly, 15, 395–423.

Deitch, M. (2006). *Effective Prison Oversight*: Prepared for the Commission on Safety and Abuse in America's Prisons, Los Angeles, California

Denhardt, R.B. (2004). *The dance of leadership.* Speech given at the 2004 ASPA Symposium, 10 Dec. in Nashville, Tenn.

Department of Public Safety, (2012). *Inmate Classification System.*

Dietz, E. F., O'Connell, D. J., and Scarpitti, F. R. (2003). *Therapeutic communities and prison management*: An examination of the effects of operating on in-prison therapeutic community levels of institutional disorder. International Journal of Offender Therapy and Comparative Criminology, 47(2), 210-223.

Dilulio, J.J. Jr. (1987). *Governing prisons*: A comparative study of correctional management. New York: The Free Press.

Donovan, N., and Halpern, D. (2002). *Life satisfaction*: The state of knowledge and implications for government. Retrieved on December 15, 2008, from http://www.number-10.gov.uk/su/ls/paper.pdf

Dumond, R.W. (2000). *Inmate Sexual Assault*: The Plague that Persists. The Prison Journal, 80(4): 407 – 414.

Dumond, R.W. (2003). *Confronting America's Most Ignored Crime Problem*: The Prison Rape Elimination Act of 2003. The Journal of the American Academy of Psychiatry and the Law, 31(3): 354 – 360.

Dvoskin, J.A., and Spiers, E.M. (2004). *On the role of correctional officers in prison mental health*. Psychiatric Quarterly, 75(1), 41-59.

Edgar, K. (2014). *Making Prisons Safe*: Prison Reform Trust.

Edgar, K. (2005). "*Conflict Resolution in Prisons*: The Cause, Prevention and Control of Prison Violence and Disorder," presented at the 14th World Congress of Criminology, Philadelphia, PA. August 11, 2005.

Edgar, K., O'Donnell, I., and Martin, C. (2003). *Prison Violence*: The dynamics of conflict, fear, and power, Cullompton: Willan Publishing.

Egley, A. Jr., Howell, J.C., and Harris, M. (2014). *Highlights of the 2012 National Youth Gang Survey*: Office of Juvenile Justice and Delinquency Prevention.

Ekland-Olson, S. (1986). "*Crowding, Social Control, and Prison Violence*: Evidence from the Post-Ruiz Years in Texas." Law and Society Review 20.3: 389-421.

English, K., Heil, P., Dumond, R. (2011). *Sexual Assault in Jail and Juvenile Facilities*: Promising Practices for Prevention and Response, Final Report. U.S. Department of Justice.

Faiver, K.L. (1998). *Health care management issues in corrections*. Lanham, MD: American Correctional Association.

Faris, R. E. (1934). *Cultural Isolation and the Schizophrenic Personal.* American Journal of Sociology, September, 40(2):155-164.

Farkas, M. A. (1995*). Correctional Officer Types: Dimensions, Relationships, and Sources*. Unpublished Doctoral Dissertation, College of Social Science, Michigan State University, Michigan.

Fellner, J. (2006). *A corrections quandary*: Mental illness and prison rules. Harvard Civil Rights–Civil Liberties Law Review, 41, 391-412.

Finn, P. (1998). *The Delaware Department of Corrections life skills program.* Washington, DC: National Institute of Justice. Office of Correctional Education, National Institute of Corrections.

Fleisher, M.S., and Decker, S.H. (2001). *An overview of the challenge of prison gangs*. Corrections Management Quarterly 5 1–9.

Flesch, R. A. (1994). *Defensive tactics for law enforcement, public safety and corrections officers*. Longwood, FL: Gould Publications.

Fong, R.S., and Buentello, S. (1991). *The detection of prison gang development*: An empirical assessment. Federal Probation, 55, 66–69.

Fong, R.S., Vogel, R.E., and Buentello, S. (1992). *Prison gang dynamics*: A look inside the Texas Department of Corrections. In P.J. Benekos and A.V. Merlo (Eds.), Corrections: Dilemmas and directions. Cincin prison culture: Prison gangs and the case of the "Pepsi generation." Social Problems, 40, 398–409.

Ford, M. (2015). *America's Largest Mental Hospital is a Jail.* The Atlantic News. Retrieved from; Http://www.theatlantic.com/politics/archive/2015/06/americas-largest-mental-hospital-is-a-jail-395012/

Forsyth, D. R. (2006). *Conflict*. In Forsyth, D. R., Group Dynamics (5th Ed.) (P. 388 - 389) Belmont: CA, Wadsworth, Cengage Learning.

Gaes, G.G, Scott C., Julianne, N., and William, S. (2004). *Measuring Prison Performance*. Walnut Creek, California: Alta Mira Press.

Gaes, G.G. (1994). "*Prison Crowding Research Reexamined.*" Prison Journal 74.3: 329364.

Gaines, L. K., and Miller, R. L. (2003). *Criminal Justice in Action* (2nd ed.). Scarborough, Ontario: Wadsworth.

Gallup Organization. (2002). *Summary of selection research item bank.*

Gaston, A. (1996). *Controlling gangs through teamwork and technology.* Large Jail Network Bulletin (Annual Issue) 7–10.

Gatotoh, A.M., Omulema, B.E.E.., and Nassiuma, D. April (2011). *Correctional Attitudes*: An Impetus for a Paradigm Shift in Inmate Rehabilitation. International Journal of Humanities and Social Science

Gerber, J., and Fritsch, E. J. (1995). *Adult academic and vocational correctional education programs*: A review of recent research. Journal of Offender Rehabilitation, 22, 119-142

Glaze, L. E., and Bonczar, T. P. (2006). *Probation and Parole in the United States, 2005.* Washington, DC: Bureau Justice Stat., U.S Dept. Justice.

Grassian, S. (1983). *Psychopathological effects of solitary confinement.* American Journal of Psychiatry, 140(11), 1450-1454.

Grassian, S. (2006). *Psychiatric Effects of Solitary Confinement*: Volume 22 Access to Justice: The Social Responsibility of Lawyers. Prison Reform: Commission on Safety and Abuse in America's Prisons.

Greenberg, E., Duleavy, E., Kutner, M., and White, S. (2007). *Literacy Behind Bars*: Results from the 2003 National Assessment of Adult Literacy

Prison Survey. http://nces.ed.gov/pubs2007/2007473. Pdf. National Center for Educational Statistics, Institute of Educational Sciences, U.S. Department of Education.

Greenberg, J. (1990a). *Organizational justice*: Yesterday, today, and tomorrow. Journal of Management, 16, 399–432.

Greenberg, J. (1990b). *Looking fair vs. being fair*: Managing impressions of organizational justice. In B. Shaw & L. Cummings (Eds.), Research in organizational behavior: 12 (pp. 111–157). Greenwich, CT: JAI Press.

Gui, A., Jafery, S.A.S., Rafiq, J., and Naeem, H. (2012). *Improving Employees Performance Through Total Quality Management*: International Journal of Economics and Management Sciences Vol. 1, No. 8, 2012, pp. 19-24

Haney, C. (2003). *Mental health issues in long-term solitary and "supermax" confinement*. Crime & Delinquency, 49(1), 124-156. DOI: 10.1177/0011128702239239.

Haney, C. (2009). *The social psychology of isolation*: Why solitary confinement is psychologically harmful. Prison Service Journal, 181, 12-20.

Harlow, C.W. (2003). *Education and Correctional Populations*. Bureau of Justice Special Report, Office of Justice Programs, U.S. Department of Justice.

Harrington, H.J. (2001). *Total Improvement Management*. McGraw-Hill, Inc, USA.

Hensley, C., Koscheski, M., and Tewksbury, R. (2005). *Examining the Characteristics of Male Sexual Assault Targets in a Southern Maximum Security Prison*. Journal of Interpersonal Violence, 20(6): 667 - 679.

Hensley, C., Tewksbury, R., and Castle, T. (2003). *Characteristics of Prison Sexual Assault Targets in Male Oklahoma Correctional Facilities*. Journal of Interpersonal Violence, 18(6): 595 – 606.

Homel, R. & Thomson, C. (2005*). Causes and prevention of violence in prisons*. In Sean O'Toole & Simon Eyland (Eds.), Corrections criminology (pp. 101-108). Sydney: Hawkins Press

Honnold, J.A., and Stinchcomb, J.B. (1985). *Officer stress*: Costs, causes, and cures. Corrections Today, 47(7): 49-50.

Horgan, G.J. (2011). The Main Areas of Inmate Litigation in the 21st

Century. http://www.corrections.com/news/article/29607-the-main-areas-of-inmate-litigation-in-the-21st-century-

Horgan, G.J. (2012). *Classification* – The Engine That Makes Correctional Facilities Go. (Classification summary)

Howells, K., Heseltine, K., Sarre, R., Davey, L. and Day, A. (2004). *Correctional Offender Rehabilitation Programs*: The National Picture in Australia

Hughes, T., and Wilson, D. J. (2002). *Reentry Trends in the United States.* Washington, D.C: Bureau Justice Stat, U.S Dept. Justice.

Huhman, H.R. (2012). *Follow The '30-60-90' Plan When Starting A New Job*: Glassdoor.

Hutchinson, V., Kristin, K., Thomas, R. (2009). *Inmate Behavior Management*: The Key to a Safe and Secure Jail: National Institute of Corrections

International Psychological Trauma Symposium. (2007) *The Istanbul statement on the use and effects of solitary confinement*: Adopted on 9th December 2007 at the International Psychological Trauma Symposium, Istanbul. Prison Service Journal, 181, 46-48.

Jackson, E.J., Ammen, S. (1996). *Race And Correctional Officers' Punitive Attitudes Toward Treatment Programs For inmates.* Journal of Criminal Justice, Vol. 24 No.2 pp.153-166, 1996.

Jackson, J., Tyler, T.R., Bradford, B., Taylor, D., Shiner, M. (2010). *Legitimacy and procedural justice in prisons*: Prison service journal (191). pp. 4-10. ISSN 0300-3558

James, D. J., and Glaze, L.E. (2006). *"Mental Health Problems of Prison and Jail Inmates."* Bureau of Justice Statistics Special Report No. NCJ 213600. Washington, DC: US Department of Justice, Office of Justice Programs

Jones and Bartlett Learning, LLC Corrections in a Changing Environment

Judge, T., and, J. (2004). *Organizational justice and stress:* The mediating role of work–family conflict. Journal of Applied Psychology, 89, 395–404.

Jurik, N.M., and Musheno, M. (1986). *The Internal Crisis of Corrections*: Professionalization and the Work Environment. Justice quarterly 3: 457-80

Karriker, J., and Williams, M. (2009). *Organizational Justice and Organi-*

zational Citizenship Behavior: A Mediated Multifoci Model†. Journal of Management, 35(1), 112.

Kiel, D.L. (2003). *The call to public service*: Entrance, learning and reflection. Public Administration Review, 63(4):498-502.

Killian, S. (MLead, MEd), (2007). *The ABC of Effective Leaders hip*: A Practical Overview of Evidence Based Leadership. Theory Australian Leadership Development Centre

Kilpatrick, D.G., Edmunds, C., Seymour, A. (1992). *Rape in America*: A report to the nation. Charleston, SC: National Victim Center & the Crime Victims Research and Treatment Center, Medical University of South Carolina

Kim, H. (2009). *"Integrating Organizational Justice into the Relationship Management Theory"*. Retrieved from Online. Available: http://www.allacademic.com/ (Retrieved from 15th of May 2009).

Kim, K., Becker-Cohen, M., Serakos, M. (2015). *Mentally Ill Persons in the Criminal Justice System*: A Scan of Practice and Background Analysis. Urban Institute.

Kimball L. S., and Nink C. E. (2006). *"How to improve employee motivation, commitment, productivity, well-being, and safety."* Corrections Today Magazine 68(3): 66-69, 74.

Konrad, A.M., and Deckop, J. (2001). *Human Resource Management trends in the USA*. Challenges in the midst of prosperity, International Journal of Manpower, vol 22, no 3, MCB University Press

Kolind, T. Frank V.A., and Dahl. H. (2010). *Drug treatment or alleviating the negative consequences of imprisonment*: A critical view of prison-based drug treatment in Denmark Volume 21, Issue 1, Pages 43-48 (January 2010)

Kratcoski, P.C. (1988). *"The Implications of Research Explaining Prison Violence and Disruption."* Federal Probation 52.1: 27-32.

Kupers, T.A. (2008). *What to do with the survivors*? Coping with the long-term effects of isolated confinement. Criminal Justice and Behavior, 35(8), 1005-1016. DOI: 10.1177/0093854808318591.

Lambert, E. (2003). *Justice in corrections*: An exploratory study of the impact of organizational justice on correctional staff. *Journal of Criminal Justice, 31*, 155– 168.

Lambert, E.G., Hogan, N.L. (2011). *Association Between Distributive and*

Procedural Justice and Life Satisfaction Among Correctional Staff: Research Note. Professional Issues in Criminal Justice Vol 6(3 & 4), 2011 31

Lariviere, M., Robinson, D. (1995). *Attitudes of Federal Correctional officers towards Offenders.* Available online at: http://www.csc-scc.gc.ca/text/rsrch/reports/r44e_e.shtml

La Vigne, N.G., Debus-Sherill, S., Brazzell, D. and Mitchell Downey, P. (2011). *Preventing Violence and sexual Assault in Jail*: A situational Crime Prevention Approach

Law, Public Safety, Corrections and Security: Emergency Plans and Procedures. Texas Education Agency, (2012). http://data.cteunt.org/content/files/law/correctional-services/unit-2-safety/2-06-emergency-plans-and-procedures/2.06-cor-emergency.pdf

Leadership, (2002). *18 Ways to Take Charge* — Fast. Fast Company. http://www.fastcompany.com/65159/18-ways-take-charge-fast

Leventhal, G. S., Karuza, J., and Fry, W. R. (1980). *Beyond fairness*: A theory of allocation preferences. In G. Mikula (Ed.), Justice and social interaction (pp. 167-218). New York: Springer-Verlag.

Liebling, A., and Shadd, M. editors. (2005). *The Effects of Imprisonment.* Portland, Oregon: Willan Publishing.

Lincoln, J., and Kalleberg, A. (1990). *Culture, control, and commitment*: A study of work organization and work attitudes in the United States and Japan. New York: Cambridge University Press.

Lind, E., and Tyler, T. (1988). *The social psychology of procedural justice.* New York: Plenum Press.

Lind, E. A., Tyler, T. R., and Huo, Y. (1997). *Procedural context and culture*: Variation in the antecedents of procedural justice judgments. Journal of Personality and Social Psychology, 73, 767- 780.

Lipsey, M.W. and Cullen, F.T. (2007). *The Effectiveness of Correctional Rehabilitation*: A Review of Systematic Reviews

Lovell, D. (2008). *Patterns of Disturbed Behavior in a Supermax Population*: Criminal Justice and Behavior, 35(8), 985-1004. DOI: 10.1177/0093854808318584.

Lucas, T. (2009). *Justifying outcomes versus processes*: Distributive and procedural justice beliefs as predictors of positive and negative affectivity. Current Psychology, 28, 249–265.

Luecke, R. (2004). *Harvard Business Essentials*: Coaching and Mentoring, Harvard Business School Press, Boston, Massachusetts.

Lygo, R. (1991). *Management of the Prison Service.* Home Office: London.

Lyman, M.D. (1989). *Gangland.* Springfield, IL: Charles C Thomas.

Mackenzie, D. L. (2006). *What Works in Corrections*? Reducing the Criminal Activities of Offenders and Delinquents. New York: Cambridge Univ. Press.

March, J., and Simon, H. A. (1958). "*Organizations*" University of Illinois at Urbana-Champaign's Academy for Entrepreneurial Leadership Historical Research Reference in Entrepreneurship.

Margo, S. (2003). *Inmate Litigation*, 116 HARV. L. REV. 1555.

Marquart, J.W., and Sorensen, J.R. eds. (1997). *Correctional contexts*: Contemporary and classical readings. Los Angeles, CA: Roxbury Pub.

Martin, M.D. and Reiss, C.L. (2008). *Managing Risk in Jails*: U.S. Department of Justice. National Institute of Corrections, NIC Accession Number 022666

Martin, M.D., Katsampes, P. (2007). *Sheriff's Guide to Effective Jail Operations*: U.S. Department of Justice, National Institute of Corrections.

Maryland Commission on Correctional Standards (MCCS): How to Prepare for an Audit. https://www.dpscs.state.md.us/publicinfo/publications/pdfs/f.pdf

Maxson, C.L., Hennigan, K.M. and Sloane, D.C. (2005). "*It's Getting Crazy Out There*: Can a Civil Gang Injunction Change a Community?" Criminology and Public Policy 4(3): 577-606.

Maxwell, J.C. (2001). *The 17 Indisputable Laws of Teamwork*: Embrace Them and Empower Your Team. Thomas Nelson, Inc. Nashville, Tennessee.

McCleery, R. (1961). *Authoritarianism and the Belief System of the Incorrigibles.* IN: Cressey, D., (ed.). The Prison. New York: Holt, Rinehart, and Winston, pp.260-306.

Ministry of Justice. (2006). *Use of Force Training Manual*: National Offender Management service.

Monahan, J. (1996). *Violence prediction*: The past twenty years and the next twenty years. Criminal Justice and Behavior, 23, 107-120.

Montgomery M. J. (2006). *"Leadership in a correctional environment."* Corrections Compendium 31(3): 1-5, 11.

Mullins, L.J. (2007). *Management and Organizational Behaviour*, 8th Edition, Financial Times, Prentice Hall, London.

Napoleon, Hill. (2013). *The Law of Success.* Penguin Group (USA), Inc.

National Commission on Correctional Health Care. (1999). *Correctional Mental Health Care*: Standards and Guidelines for Delivering Services. Chicago: National Commission on Correctional Health Care

National Council of Nonprofits: Step 2: Preparing for the Audit, Nonprofit Audit Guide. https://www.councilofnonprofits.org/nonprofit-audit-guide/preparing-for-audit

National Prison Rape Elimination Commission Report. (2009).

National Standards to Prevent, Detect, and Respond to Prison Rape: Department of Justice

NIC. (2013). *How can our agency prepare for a PREA audit?* http://nicic.gov/topics/5215-how-can-our-agency-prepare-for-a-prea-audit

O'Donnell, I., and Edgar, K. (1996). *The Extent and Dynamics of Victimization in Prison.* Oxford, U.K.: Centre for Criminological Research, Oxford University.

O'Hara, C. (2014). *What New Team Leaders Should Do First*: Harvard Business Review. https://hbr.org/2014/09/what-new-team-leaders-should-do-first

Ohio Department of Rehabilitation and Correction: What Works? General Principles, Characteristics, and Examples of Effective Programs

Ombudsman New South Wales. (2012). *Managing use of Force in Prisons*: The Need for Better Policy and Practice. A Special Report to Parliament under s.31 of the Ombudsman Act 1974 (2012).

Osterstuck, G. (2012). *Don't Let Inmate Lawsuits Affect Your Job.* http://www.corrections.com/news/article/30722-don-t-let-inmate-lawsuits-affect-your-job

Parker, G. (2006). *Mental illness in jails & prisons*: An overview for correctional staff. Retrieved April 9, 2008, from http://www.in.gov/indcorrection/news/030106suicidesummitjailsprisons.ppt

Pastore, A., and Maguire, K. (Eds.). (2007). *Sourcebook of criminal justice statistics* [Electronic version]. Retrieved December 12, 2007, from http://www.albany.edu/sourcebook/

Patterson, M., West, M., Lawthom, R., and Nickell, S. (1997*). Impact of People Management Practices on Business Performance.* London: Institute of Personnel and Development.

Pennsylvania Coalition Against Rape. (2006). *Meeting the Needs of Prison Rape Victims*: A Technical Assistance Guide for Sexual Assault Counselors and Advocates

Phillips, J.M. (1998). *Effects of realistic job previews on multiple organizational outcomes*: A meta-analysis. Academy of Management Journal, 41, 673–690.

Pillay, N., Dawood, Q., and Karodia, A.M. (2015).*The Relationship Between Career Development and Staff Motivation in the South African Petroleum Sector*: A Case Study of A Durban Refinery: Arabian Journal of Business and Management Review (Nigerian Chapter) Vol. 3. No 2. 2015.

Piotrowski, K. (2009). *The Career Coward's Guide to Career Advancement*: sensible strategies for overcoming career fear

Pope, L. G., Hopper, K., Davis, C., Cloud, D. (2016). *First-Episode Incarceration*: Creating a Recovery-Informed Framework for Integrated Mental Health and Criminal Justice Responses. Vera Institute of Justice.

PREA Data Collection Activities. (2015). U.S. Department of Justice, Office of Justice Programs. Bureau of Statistics.

Prison Reform Trust. (2014). *Prison*: The Facts – Bromley Briefings, Summer 2014 http://www.prisonreformtrust.org.uk/Portals/0/Documents/Prison%20the%20facts%20May%202014.pdf

Prison Service Order (PSO) 1600. (2015). *Use of Force*: HM Prison Service.

Ralph, P. H., & Marquart, J. W. (1992). *Gang violence in Texas prisons. The Prison Journal,* 71 38–49.

Raţiu, P., Mortan, M., Lazar, I. (2011). *Using 360-degree feedback for improving employee's* performance. Different perspectives - an overview, Revista Economică, no 3 (56), Sibiu, pp 341-350.

Reaves, B.A. (2012). *Hiring and Retention of State and Local Law Enforcement Officers*, 2008– Statistical Tables. Bureau of Justice Statistics

Reising, M., and Lovrich, N. (1998). *Job attitudes Among Higher – Custody State Prison Management Personnel*: A Cross – Sectional Comparative Assessment, Journal of Criminal Justice, Vol. 26, No 3, pp213-226.

Richard, P. J., Devinney, T.M., Yip, G.S. and Johnson, G. (2009).

Measuring Organizational Performance: Towards Methodological Best Practice: Journal of Management

Robbins, I.P. Project Guide: Objective Classification Analysis. Native American and Alaskan Technical Assistance Project

Robbins, I.P. (2008). Lessons from Hurricane Katrina: Prison Emergency Preparedness as a Constitutional Imperative. American University Washington College of Law.

Robbins, T., Summers, T., Miller, J., and Hendrix, W. (2000). *Using the group-value model to explain the role of non-instrumental justice in distinguishing the effects of distributive and procedural justice.* Journal of Occupational and Organizational Psychology, 73, 511–518.

Robertson, J.E. (2003). *Rape Among Incarcerated Men*: Sex, Coercion, and STDs. AIDS Patient Care and STDs, 17(8): 423 – 430

Robinson, D., Porporino, F., and Simourd, L. (1997). *The influence of educational attainment on the attitudes and job performance of correctional Officers.* Crime and delinquency, 4 3 (1), 60-77.

Rothstein, M., and Stannow, L. (2009). *Improving Prison Oversight to Address Sexual Violence in Detention. American Constitution Society for Law and Policy.*

Ruback, R. B., and Carr, T. S. (1993). "*Prison Crowding Over Time;* The Relationship of Density and Changes in Density to Infraction Rates." Criminal Justice and Behavior, 20, 130-148.

Rubery, R. (1997). *Wages and the Labor Market*: British Journal of Industrial Relations, 35 (3): 337-362.

Ryan, J. Dealing with the Mentally Ill and Emotionally Disturbed in the Use of Force Context: Public Agency Training Council. http://www.patc.com/weeklyarticles/uof_mentallyill.shtml

Rynes, S. L., and Cable, D.M. (2003). *Recruitment research in the twenty-first century.* In W. C. Borman D. R. Ilgen and R. J. Klimoski (Eds.), Handbook of psychology: Industrial and organizational psychology, vol. 12. (pp. 55–76)Hoboken, NJ: John Wiley & Sons.

Saari, L. M., and Judge, T. A. (2004). *Employee attitudes and job satisfaction.* Human Resource Management. Wiley.

Schlanger, M. (2003). *Inmate Litigation*, 116 HARV. L. REV. 1555.

Schmalleger, F., and Smykla, J.O. (2001). *Corrections in the 21st Century.* New York: McGraw-Hill.

Schoenly, L. (2014). *4 Tips for Handling Mentally Ill Inmates*: Correctional Healthcare. http://www.correctionsone.com/officer-safety/articles/7453157-4-tips-for-handling-mentally-ill-inmates/

Schwartz, J.A. and Barry, C. (1996). *Critical Analysis of Emergency Preparedness*: Self-Audit Materials, National Institute of Corrections.

Schwartz, J.A., Barry, C. (2005). *A Guide to Preparing for and Responding to Prison Emergencies*: Self-Audit Checklists • National Survey Results • Resource Materials • Case Studies. LETRA, Inc. Campbell, California.

Schwartz, J. A. and Barry, C. (2005). *A Guide to Preparing for and Responding to Prison Emergencies*: LETRA, Inc. Campbell, California

Schwartz, J. A. and Barry, C. (2009). *A Guide to Preparing for and Responding to Jail Emergencies*: National Institute of Corrections. LETRA, Inc. Campbell, CA.

Scott, G.D., and Gendreau, P. (1969). *Psychiatric Implications of Sensory Deprivation in a Maximum Security Prison.* Canadian Psychiatric Association Journal, 14(1):337-341.

Shalev, S. (2008). *A sourcebook on solitary confinement:* Mannheim Center for Criminology. Produced with the assistance of the Nuffield Foundation.

Smith, P.S. (2008) "*Degenerate criminals*": Mental health and psychiatric studies of Danish prisoners in solitary confinement, 1870-1920. Criminal Justice and Behavior, 35(8), 1048-1064. DOI: 10.1177/0093854808318782.

Steedman, H., and Wagner, K. (1989). *Productivity, Machinery and Skills*: Clothing Manufacture in Britain and Germany, National Institute Economic Review, May: 40-57

Stewart. G.L., and Brown, K.G. (2011). *Improving Employee Performance, chapter in Human Resource Management* – linking strategy to practice, second edition, John Wiley & Sons, Inc. available at: http://avaxhome.ws/ebooks/business_job/0470530499 Human Manage.html

Stinchcomb, J.B., McCampbell, S.W., and Layman, E.P. (2006). *Future Force.* A Guide to Building The 21st Century Community Corrections Workforce. National Institute of Corrections, Center for Innovative Public Policies, Inc.

Stohr M.K., C. Hemmens M. Kifer., and M. Schoeler. (2000). *We know it, we just have to do it*: Perceptions of ethical work in prisons and jails. The Prison Journal, 80(2): 126-150.

Stohr, M. K., and Zupan, L. L. (1992). *Street-level Bureaucrats and Service Provision in Jails*: The failure of Officers to Identify the Needs of Inmates. American Journal of Criminal Justice, Volume XVI, Number 2.

Sundram, C.J. (1999). *Quality Assurance for Mental Health Services in Correctional Facilities*. Correctional Mental Health Report, 1 (1), 5.

Sutherland, E.H., and Cressey, D.R. (1955). *Principles of criminology*, 5th Ed. New York: J.B. Lippincott Company.

Taxman, F., and Gordon, J. (2009). *Do fairness and equity matter*? An examination of organizational justice among correctional officers in adult prisons. Criminal Justice and Behavior, 36, 695–711.

Teeters, N. K. (1955). *The cradle of the penitentiary*. Philadelphia: Pennsylvania Prison Society.

The National Gang Report (2013). National Gang Intelligence Center.

The Use of Force Training Manual. (2006). *HM Prison Service Training & Development Group*: Ministry of Justice

Thornberry, T.P., Marvin, D.K., Alan, J.L., Carolyn A.S., and Kimberly, T. (2003). *Gangs and Delinquency in Developmental Perspective*. Cambridge, U.K.: Cambridge University Press.

Toch, H. (1992). *Living in prison*: The ecology of survival. Washington, DC: American Psychological Association

Toch, H., and Klofas, J. (1982). *Alienation and Desire for Job Enrichment Among Correctional Officers*. Federal Probation, 46, 35-44.

Toch, H. (2008). *Cumulative default*: The cost of disruptive prison careers. Criminal Justice and Behavior, 35(8), 943-955. DOI: 10.1177/0093854808318594.

Travis, J. (2005). *But They All Come Back*. Washington, D.C.: The Urban Institute Press.

Treatment Advocacy Center. (2007). *Criminalization of individual with severe psychiatric disorders*. Retrieved April 9, 2008, from http://www.treatmentadvocacycenter.org/GeneralResources/Fact3.htm

Trulson, C.R., Marquart, J.W., and Kawucha, S.K. (2008). *Gang Suppression and Institutional Control*: Corrections.com. Reprinted with permission of the American Correctional Association, Alexandria, Va. http://www.correctionsone.com/prison-gangs/articles/1842642-Gang-suppression-and-institutional-control/

Tyler, T. R., and Huo, Y. J. (2002). *Trust in the Law*: Encouraging

Public Cooperation with the Police and Courts. New York: Russell Sage Foundation.

Tyler, T. R. (2007). *Psychology and the Design of Legal Institutions.* Nijmegen, The Netherlands: Wolf.

Tyler, T. R. (2008). '*Psychology and Institutional Design*', Review of Law and Economics, 4, 6.

United Nations. (2015). *Handbook on Dynamic Security and Prison Intelligence*: English, Publishing and Library Section, United Nations Office at Vienna.

https://en.wikipedia.org/wiki/Prison_escape

United Nations. (2013). *Prison Incident Management Handbook*: Corrections.

https://www.griffith.edu.au/__data/assets/pdf_file/0003/188706/causes2.pdf

http://solitarywatch.com/wp-content/uploads/2011/01/cost-of-long-term-isolation1.pdf http://openscholarship.wustl.edu/cgi/viewcontent.cgi?article=1348&context=law_journal_law_policy http://openscholarship.wustl.edu/cgi/viewcontent.cgi?article=1362&context=law_journal_law_policy

University Alliance, What Makes an Effective Leader. Mendoza College of Business, University of Notre Dame.http://www.notredameonline.com/resources/leadership-and-management/what-makes-an-effective-leader/#.V4o-bW6EDIU

UNODC. (2010). *Handbook for Prison Leaders*: A basic training tool and curriculum for prison managers based on international standards and norms. Criminal Justice Handbook Series, United Nations Publication

VanDevender, T. (Retrieved on 18th Dec. 2011). Total Quality Human Resources Management: http://www.freequality.org/documents/knowledge/Total%20 Quality%20Human%20Resource%20Management pdf.

Van Voorhis, P., and Kelly, Brown. (1995). *Evaluability Assessment*: A Tool for Program Development in Corrections. Washington, D.C.: National Institute of Corrections (P.O. #6012).

Visher, C., and Courtney, S. (2007). *Cleveland Prisoners' Experiences Returning Home*. Washington D.C.: The Urban Institute Justice Policy Center.

Wakefield, D. (1980). *A Thousand Days of Solitary.* London: National Prisoners' Movement (PROP).

Walters, S.T., Clark, M.D., Gingerich R., Meltzer, M.L. (2007). *A guide for probation and parole*: Motivating offenders to change available http://www.doc.state.nc.us/dcc/EBP/guideforprobationmotivatchgnic.pdf

Watts, T. Why Career Development Matters: Careers England

Weiss, B. (2013). "*4 Simple Career Advancement Strategies,*" money.usnews.com, http://money.usnews.com/money/blogs/outside-voices-careers/2013/05/07/4-simple-tips-for-obtaining-professional-bliss

Williamsburg VA. (2003). *Author National Association for Court Management Leadership*: What this core competency is and why it is important.

https://en.wikipedia.org/wiki/Procedural_justice

Wilson, D. B., Gallagher, C. A., Coggeshall, M. B., and MacKenzie, D. L. (1999). *A quantitative review and description of corrections based education, vocation, and work programs.* Corrections Management Quarterly, 3, 8-18.

Wilson, D. B., Gallagher, C. A., and Mackenzie, D. L. (2000). *A meta-analysis of corrections-based education, vocation, and work programs for adult offenders.* Journal of Research on Crime and Delinquency, 37, 347-368.

Wortley, R. (2002*). Situational Prison Control*: Crime Prevention in Correctional Institutions. Cambridge, UK: Cambridge University Press

Wrenn, P. (2013). "*Want to Advance Your Career?* Seek Out a Sponsor," forbes.com, http://www.forbes.com/sites/learnvest/2013/10/08/want-to-advance-your-career-seek-out-a-sponsor

Wright, N.K. (2005). *"Designing a National Performance Measurement System"* The Prison Journal 85(3): 368-393.

Young, L. J., Antonio, M.E., and Wingeard. (2009). *How staff attitude and support for inmate treatment and rehabilitation differs by job category:* An evaluation of findings from Pennsylvania's Department of Corrections' employee training curriculum 'Reinforcing Positive Behavior' Journal of Criminal Justice Volume 37, Issue 5, September-October 2009, Pages 435-441

Zweig, J.M., Naser, R.L., Blackmore, J. and Schaffer, M. (2007). *Addressing Sexual Violence in Prisons*: A National Snapshot of Approaches and Highlights of Innovative Strategies, Final Report

About The Author

Elvis Slaughter is a criminal justice and law enforcement expert that has several years of experience in criminology. Embracing the core values of effective leadership enabled him to excel in his career. Slaughter served the Cook County jail complex that often exceeds ten thousand inmates in various capacities— beginning as an officer and deputy sheriff at the Cook County Sheriff's Office and rising to Superintendent of Corrections— before retiring in 2009. Slaughter's intuitive understanding of criminal behavior, dedication to managing correctional facility operations, passion for rehabilitating detainees, and systems approach to organizational management played a vital role in running correctional divisions with a high level of effectiveness, especially during his leadership roles. While employed at the Cook County Sheriff's Office, he also served as an Intern Investigator for the Cook County Public Defender's Office, President of the Illinois Academy of Criminology, consultant, writer, and public speaker.

Slaughter is also an Educator, Auditor for the American Correctional Association and currently serves as Lansing Fire and Police Commissioner. Slaughter earned an associate's degree in Electronics Engineering, a bachelor's degree, and a master's degree in Criminal Justice and Corrections. Slaughter is the recipient of numerous awards, including the prestigious Thrasher Award from the National Gang Crime Research Center. Slaughter also enjoys crafting works of fiction and non-fiction based on his extensive criminology experience. During his free time, Slaughter volunteers his time to community work, public speaking, and mentoring the next generation.

www.ingramcontent.com/pod-product-compliance
Lightning Source LLC
Chambersburg PA
CBHW031219290326
41931CB00035B/300
* 9 7 8 0 9 9 6 5 9 3 2 5 0 *